MW00474760

Wong Kar-wai |

Contemporary Film Directors

Edited by James Naremore

The Contemporary Film Directors series provides concise, well-written introductions to directors from around the world and from every level of the film industry. Its chief aims are to broaden our awareness of important artists, to give serious critical attention to their work, and to illustrate the variety and vitality of contemporary cinema. Contributors to the series include an array of internationally respected critics and academics. Each volume contains an incisive critical commentary, an informative interview with the director, and a detailed filmography.

A list of books in the series appears
at the end of this book.

Wong Kar-wai |

Peter Brunette

**UNIVERSITY
OF
ILLINOIS
PRESS**
URBANA
AND
CHICAGO

Library of Congress Cataloging-in-Publication Data
Brunette, Peter.
Wong Kar-wai / Peter Brunette.
p.   cm. — (Contemporary film directors)
Includes transcripts of interviews with Wong Kar-wai.
Filmography: p. 135
Includes bibliographical references and index.
ISBN 0-252-02992-5 (alk. paper)
ISBN 978-0-252-02992-9 (alk. paper)
ISBN 0-252-07237-5 (pbk. : alk. paper)
ISBN 978-0-252-07237-6 (pbk. : alk. paper)
1. Wong, Kar-wai, 1958—Criticism and interpretation.
I. Wong, Kar-wai, 1958– II. Title. III. Series.
PN1998.3.W65B78   2005
791.4302'33'092—dc22   2004020467

Frontispiece: Wong Kar-wai (left) on the set of
In the Mood for Love with his director of photography,
Christopher Doyle. © 2000 USA Films. All rights reserved.

To my wife, Lynne Johnson, now more than ever. And she knows why.

Contents |

Figure 1. ©1988 The Film Reference Library. All rights reserved. http://www.filmreferencelibrary.ca.

Figure 2. ©1991 The Film Reference Library. All rights reserved. http://www.filmreferencelibrary.ca.

Figure 3. ©1994 The Film Reference Library. All rights reserved. http://www.filmreferencelibrary.ca.

Figure 4. ©1994 The Film Reference Library. All rights reserved. http://www.filmreferencelibrary.ca.

Figure 5. ©1994 The Film Reference Library. All rights reserved. http://www.filmreferencelibrary.ca.

Figure 6. ©1994 The Film Reference Library. All rights reserved. http://www.filmreferencelibrary.ca.

Figure 7. ©1994 The Film Reference Library. All rights reserved. http://www.filmreferencelibrary.ca.

Figure 8. ©1995 Kino International. All rights reserved.

Figure 9. ©1995 Kino International. All rights reserved.

Figure 10. ©1995 Kino International. All rights reserved.

I saw my first Wong Kar-wai film in 1995 at the Toronto International Film Festival. It was *Fallen Angels,* and I was overwhelmed. Who was this amazing filmmaker with such a brilliant new visual style? I stumbled, still dazed, into the Sutton Place Hotel, the festival's headquarters at the time, and ran into James Quandt, the longtime director of the Ontario Cinémathèque and a man of impeccable cinematic taste. "I've just seen the future of cinema," I said breathlessly. In his usual low-key manner, James replied, "Oh, you're just coming from the Wong Kar-wai film?"

Nearly a decade later, Wong's signature visual pyrotechnics don't wield quite as much power over me as they once did, but this is only to be expected. The best news is that Wong has matured as a filmmaker, and where sheer visual and aural audacity was once enough to thrill a viewer, these ephemeral techniques—ephemeral if they're not ultimately backed up by something more substantial—have, in more recent films like *Happy Together* and *In the Mood for Love,* been supplemented by a powerful artistic vision and a new depth of feeling.

Though this may scandalize some, I must admit immediately that I don't care for most Hong Kong cinema, especially that of the martial arts, shoot-'em-up variety, which sometimes seems to be most of it. I acknowledge its worldwide success. I appreciate its unbounded energy and its often exciting joie de vivre. I understand the arguments made by David Bordwell and others for the wonderful balletic kinesthesia and the fecund and often extremely clever recycling of generic motifs from pop culture that can be found in Hong Kong cinema. I respect the tremendous influence that Hong Kong genre films have had on Wong's filmmaking—an influence that is traced in this study—but I also believe that his greatest triumphs have come when he has transcended generic conventions. I don't want to make a value judgment that Wong's films are "better" than such generic classics as, say, *Police Story* and *Bullet in the Head;* I only want to claim that they are different and, to me at least, finally more interesting.

I also recognize that to prefer "art" films to formula films expresses a covert aesthetic position that may not ultimately be justifiable, as Jane Feuer has succinctly put it: "It was assumed that genre films could not have any artistic merit, because they were not original works and because they were not authored works. These standards of evaluation are based upon a romantic theory of art that places the highest value on the concepts of originality, personal creativity, and the idea of individual artist as genius" (142). I hope that my admiration for Wong's films is not based on simplistic ideas of genius and originality, which Feuer rightly calls into question, but rather on an irresistible attraction to depth and complexity. Frankly, I just get bored watching all that slow-motion martial arts stuff and all those endless gunfights, interrupted occasionally by the most appalling sentimentality. Wong's films seem to offer more.

This debate is intensified by the political valence it inevitably entails. Curtis K. Tsui rightly complains that Wong has "even been accused—as if this were a damning trait—of being 'European' in his aesthetic. It's an odd statement to be sure; the complaint seems to imply that, because his style is unconventional (in relation to most Hong Kong cinema), he is to be immediately disregarded as a director of 'Hong Kong films,' and that one must immediately equate 'European' and 'arthouse film' as synonymous terminology" (93). Tsui's own placement of Wong's films is unequivocal:

> [T]he fact is that Wong is one of the most distinctly "Chinese" of the Hong Kong directors working today, both in his aesthetic and in his narrative/thematic concerns. He often combines with Western filmmaking techniques various formal elements that are similar to those found in classical Taoist scroll painting: a monochromatic palette, a stressing of the work's location/setting, multifocal perspectives for the observer, and imagistic representation and emotionally expressive visuals rather than directly-stated narratives and characterizations. (94)

Though my approach in this book relies on European formal aesthetics (owing to my own lamentable lack of knowledge regarding Chinese aesthetics) and political questions that are perhaps universal, Tsui's enumeration of the specifically Chinese qualities of Wong's films is useful and revealing.

Tsui gets another thing right when he says that "in Wong's case particularly, form is the essence of his films—it is, in many ways, the narrative of his work. . . . It's not a case of style over substance; rather, it's style as substance" (94). Larry Gross, one of Wong's earliest and most sensitive western critics, makes a related argument for the director's specialness: "In fact, no less than an Antonioni or a Welles, Wong Kar-wai's deepest interest is in creating an original mode of cinematic narration. Image, actor movement and language are all unleashed to usurp the authority of straightforward linear narrative, but this turns out to have very specific thematic and formal applications and implications" (8).

I wholeheartedly agree with these views, and much of what follows in this book could be seen as an elaboration of the insights of Tsui and Gross. But, in addition to Wong's recurrent themes of time, love, and loss, I want to emphasize especially the graphic expressivity of so much of what Wong does, which was also an important concern in my previous book on the Italian director Michelangelo Antonioni and is what attracted me to Wong's films in the first place. Though our language to describe this graphic expressivity is crude, I want to focus on the way Wong's films signify in formal visual terms. In addition, I hope to say something useful about the music in Wong's films, which has been largely neglected. I believe that music—and sound in general—is a crucial feature of these films that actually "activates" much of what is visually brilliant in them.

To my mind, this search for a new way to tell cinematic stories makes Wong a postmodernist filmmaker of the first order. Others do not agree. Tony Rayns, an astute British commentator on Asian cinema, has said that "although [Wong] draws on many and disparate sources in his films, *he is never a postmodernist bricoleur.* His work deals with primary emotions, not secondary echoes of emotions; he cares about feelings, not cultural gestures" ("Charisma" 36). I wonder if anyone is still (or ever was) capable of bypassing "cultural gestures" to get to "primary emotions." In fact, Wong's later films, especially the sublime *In the Mood for Love,* specifically explore the impossibility of making such a distinction. In any case, "postmodern" is a label that is rapidly losing its explanatory power, if it ever had any, and the distinction doesn't seem as crucial as it once did.

What is especially attractive about Wong's films is what might be called their "mysterization" of everyday life, in the manner, perhaps, of the late Polish director Krzysztof Kieslowski rather than Godard, to whom he is often mistakenly compared. Some critics have described this as an emphasis on creating mood rather than emotion, but it's more than this, because the mood always seems both unspecifiable and exact at the same time. This mysterization is achieved by employing sound and visuals in ways that few directors have managed, ways that transcend the norms of contemporary international cinema, which still relies heavily on narration, dialogue, and conventional drama. Wong's films are sometimes dismissed because they are all "surface" with no depth, and it is precisely this new way of expressing meaning that will be my focus throughout this modest study. His depth, and thus the real source of his power, can be found on the surface.

||||

To rehearse the sketchiest of biographical details: Wong Kar-wai was born in Shanghai in 1958 and moved with his family to Hong Kong when he was five years old. As Stephen Teo has pointed out, Wong's personal trajectory duplicates the movement of Hong Kong cinema itself, which had its commercial and aesthetic roots in the vibrant Shanghai film industry that was displaced by the Japanese occupation in 1937 and the communist victory in 1949 (4). Originally attracted to the graphic arts, Wong studied at Hong Kong Polytechnic before specializing in television and film production at the school run by HKTVB, one of Hong Kong's biggest television stations. Fully inserted into the local film industry, he wrote a number of scripts for soap operas such as "Don't Look Now" (1981), as well as sitcoms, television films, and films destined for theatrical release, including Frankie Chan's *Just for Fun* (1983), Jeff Lau's *The Haunted Cop Shop of Horrors* (1987), and Patrick Tam's legendary if rarely seen *Final Victory* (1987), before being allowed to make his feature-film directorial debut with *As Tears Go By* in 1988. Amazingly, this film was selected by the Directors' Fortnight section at the Cannes Film Festival for presentation in 1989. Perhaps owing to the rigors of this apprenticeship, Wong has since said that he "hates" writing because shooting from a finished script is "boring." To the dismay of his actors, instead of writing scripts, he writes his films in segments, often faxing pages of dialogue to actors from his hotel room just before they are to shoot a scene.

In 1991, Wong went on to make the more personal and more self-consciously "artistic" film *Days of Being Wild*, before becoming involved in a magnificent, claustrophobic, epic historical drama called *Ashes of Time*, which took two years to film and has only been infrequently seen since it came out in 1994. Next came *Chungking Express*, a bit of fun made from start to finish in only three months, while on hiatus from *Ashes of Time*, which ironically catapulted Wong to international attention when Miramax released it in the United States in 1995. The underrated *Fallen Angels* (1995), a kind of companion piece to *Chungking Express*, came next and was released in the United States in 1997. Though these films for the most part deal with ultracool, alienated Hong Kong twentysomething heterosexuals, Wong's next film, the superb and ironically titled *Happy Together*, which premiered at Cannes in 1997, focuses on two gay Hong Kong lovers adrift in Buenos Aires and marks a new stage in his artistic development. After a shoot that lasted fifteen grueling months, Wong's masterpiece, *In the Mood for Love*, appeared in 2000, having been completed the morning of its premiere in the competition at Cannes.

Though they have rarely been commercially successful on his home turf, Wong's films have won innumerable awards in Hong Kong and, more recently, elsewhere. In 1994, *Ashes of Time* won the cinematography prize at the Venice Film Festival, and in 1997, Wong won for best director at Cannes for *Happy Together*. His frequent lead actor, Tony Leung Chiu-wai, was named best actor at Cannes in 2000 for his performance in *In the Mood for Love*. Along with the commercials and music videos he continues to make to keep busy, his current project is the eagerly awaited *2046*, part of which is set fifty years after the handover of Hong Kong to mainland China. This brilliant and exciting director obviously has many more great films ahead of him. Consider this merely an interim report.

| | |

Several people and organizations have been crucial to the completion of this book. I want to thank Joan Catapano of the University of Illinois Press and James Naremore, editor of this exciting and long-overdue series, for asking me to participate. They are valued even more as friends than as colleagues. I appreciate the time and effort generously expended by Gary Palmucci of Kino International, Barbara Scharres of the Gene Siskel Film Center of the School of the Art Institute of Chicago, and Eve Goldin of the Film Reference Library of the Toronto International Film Festival Group in helping me locate and acquire still photographs of Wong's films. I am also deeply grateful to Gilles Ciment and the Cannes Film Festival for permission to reprint Gilles's illuminating 2001 interview with Wong Kar-wai that took place under the rubric of "Leçon de Cinéma" at that year's festival. I was present, and it was thrilling. And to my graduate research assistant, the long-suffering Matt Condon, I extend my gratitude for the excellent job he did transcribing and editing the two interviews as well as for his work putting the filmography together. (Note: All translations, except where indicated, are my own.)

Wong Kar-wai |

Tears, Time, and Love:
The Films of Wong Kar-wai

As Tears Go By

In 1988, when Wong Kar-wai directed his first film, *As Tears Go By*, he had already been working in the Hong Kong film industry for a number of years, principally as a scriptwriter. The project was initially given to Wong as a star vehicle for Andy Lau, a popular singer at the time (Carbon 36), initiating a pattern that has continued throughout the director's career. In an interview with the French journal *Positif*, whose critics were early supporters of Wong's films, the director explained that *As Tears Go By* was originally intended to be the second film in a trilogy: "The first part hasn't (yet) been filmed. The third is *Final Victory*, directed by Patrick Tam [and written by Wong], when the gangster is in his thirties and realizes that he hasn't been successful. In *As Tears Go By*, the second part, he's in his twenties. In the first part, which would have been called 'Hero for a Day,' he would be an adolescent" (Ciment, "Entretien" 40). Given the fact that the gangster hero dies at the end of

Figure 1. *As Tears Go By*: Fly (left, Jacky Cheung) recklessly challenges a ruthless gang boss.

As Tears Go By, however, the narrative logic of Wong's proposed trilogy is not entirely clear.

In this putative middle film, Ah Wah (Andy Lau) is a young gangster who is torn between emotional commitments to his irresponsible friend, Fly (Jacky Cheung), and his cousin, Ah Ngor (Maggie Cheung), with whom he falls in love when she comes for a visit. After numerous confrontations with assorted bad guys that explosively punctuate the sparse narrative, Wah leaves the thug life to pursue the healthier and more fulfilling relationship that Ngor offers him. Inevitably, Fly pulls him back to Mongkok, an unsavory part of Kowloon, into the dangerously macho world of honor and betrayal that he is trying to escape. Fly is intent upon making a name for himself within triad circles by assassinating an informer held by the police, while Wah is just as intent on protecting his "little brother." At the end of the film, both tragically meet their deaths.

Wong told another French critic that he had remarkable freedom in the making of *As Tears Go By:* "At the time, because of the success of John Woo's *A Better Tomorrow* (1986), gangster films were doing very well and, as a new director, I wanted to do one too, but different from what I had seen in Hong Kong. I wanted to do a film about *young* gangsters. And since I knew the producer very well, he gave me lots of freedom" (Reynaud, "Entretien" 37).

This focus on young gangsters has led many critics to exaggerate the connection between Wong's first film and the American director Martin Scorsese's feature debut, *Mean Streets* (1973). Wong discussed this apparent linkage with Michel Ciment: "I think the Italians have lots of things in common with the Chinese: their values, their sense of friendship, their Mafia, their pasta, their mother. When I saw *Mean Streets* for the first time, it was a shock because I had the impression that the story could just as easily have taken place in Hong Kong." However, Wong went on to say, he actually only borrowed the Robert DeNiro character from Scorsese's film, since the other characters came from his own experience (Ciment, "Entretien" 41).

According to the director, the source of the specific details of *As Tears Go By* lies in his spending night after night in bars with a gangster friend. "We knew someone who didn't know a word of English but who had a British girlfriend who worked in a bar: she kept leaving him and then coming right back. They were a strange couple who didn't communicate at all. That also inspired the character in the film. So I spent three or four years of my youth drinking, fighting, and driving fast cars" (Ciment, "Entretien" 41).

The central critical debate around *As Tears Go By*—in retrospect, of course, since the film was barely noticed by western critics when it first appeared in 1988—concerns its relation to the dominant tradition of Hong Kong genre films. Is it primarily another example of a generic gangster film, in the tradition made famous by John Woo and others? Or is it an altogether new beast, an art film from Hong Kong that bears the unmistakable imprint of an auteur interested in moving beyond genre?[1]

Each side has its partisans. In the genre camp, David Bordwell has argued, rather implausibly, that it is the generic origins of Wong's films that "have international appeal in a period when directors are encouraged to make crossovers. However idiosyncratic Wong's films are, they take popular norms as points of departure" (*Planet* 270). Generically speaking, it's clear that some elements of Wong's first film are outright borrowings from previous Hong Kong movies. For example, as Bordwell points out, the café killing, "with bodies writhing against taut plastic curtains," seems to hark back to Ringo Lam's *City on Fire* (270). Nevertheless, it's a stretch to claim that Wong's links to genre are the primary attraction for his growing international audience, an audience that seems to especially appreciate his later films for their art-film qualities. Those art-film lovers who have come to deeply admire his work are not necessarily fans of more traditional Hong Kong films.

If we are intent on inscribing Wong's films within a generic rubric, it is important to remember that they share generic links with other films, from other countries, that were made long before John Woo or Tsui Hark came on the scene. As the Austrian critic Andreas Ungerböck has pointed out, *As Tears Go By* is indeed part of a genre—"gangster melodrama"—that goes back at least as far as Hollywood in the thirties (25). Ungerböck correctly insists that "gangsters in love, as everyone knows since Howard Hawks' *Scarface* (1932), are careless and distracted. And Ah Wah is tired, tired of the fighting and tired of hanging on. And in this he doesn't at all follow the larger-than-life heroes of John Woo" (25).

Chuck Stephens, an American critic, represents the antigeneric camp. He has insisted that Wong's "interest in formulas—other than the one he's in the process of inventing himself—is virtually nonexistent" (15). Going further than Stephens, J. Carbon believes that even an early film like *As Tears Go By* represents the complete repudiation of Woo's film noir heroes, who are based on the classic Chinese heroes trapped by the rigors of a masculine code that pushes them to masochism. For Carbon, the film "turns its back in an insolent manner on the tradition of the local heroic cinema" (36).

Carbon overstates his case—Wong's film is clearly enamored of its romantic gangster hero, most of whose problems do, in fact, stem from a masochistic masculine code—but he is right to claim that Woo and Wong differ most obviously in what might be called the "femininized" nature of the latter's films. As Carbon rather dramatically puts it, "*As Tears Go By* is a film that dares to be tender, a film of hidden tenderness made by a hugely timid man, a poet who wants to make of women superb and fragile beings, idealized incarnations of the traditional Chinese woman (perhaps his sole concession to classicism). Where John Woo imposes the idea of a *yang* cinema, Wong will always definitively be *yin*" (36).

To some extent, this debate is entirely beside the point, because, as the director explained to Anthony Kaufman, the division between art and genre film is hardly clear: "In Hong Kong in the '6os, going to cinema was a big thing. We have cinemas for Hollywood films, local productions, European cinema, but there was no [label of] art film at that time. Even Fellini was treated as a commercial film. So as a kid, I spent a lot of time with my mother in the cinemas. And we didn't know which is an art film, which is a commercial film, we just liked to watch the cinema."

Nevertheless, critical writing requires distinctions, and it makes sense to see Wong as still thoroughly involved in generic filmmaking in *As Tears Go By*, yet clearly at the same time embarked on a counter-trajectory that will come to fruition in succeeding films, when he begins to leave genre definitively behind. Wong himself signaled a clear division between this first film and what was to follow in an interview with Ungerböck recorded some years later: "I could have continued making films like *As Tears Go By* for the rest of eternity but I wanted to do something more personal after that. I wanted to break the structure of the average Hong Kong film" (26).

Despite Carbon's claim that *As Tears Go By* is resolutely antiheroic, the film's triad milieu is clearly glamorized throughout, as is Ah Wah, its protagonist. Part of this fawning treatment is actually unrelated to genre and stems from an unembarrassed affection for twentysomethings in love that is not totally out of place in a self-conscious filmmaker who was twenty-nine years old when the film was made. Here, at least, Bordwell's charge that Wong's is "a deeply sentimental cinema" is true. But we needn't automatically agree that this is a wholly bad thing, nor assent to this critic's somewhat condescending conclusion: "Almost devoid of irony, Wong's films, like classic rock and roll, take seriously all the crushes, the posturing, and the stubborn capriciousness of young angst. They rejoice in manic expenditures of energy. They celebrate the momentary heartbreak of glimpsing a stranger who might be interesting to love" (*Planet* 281).

Though it becomes more obvious as Wong's career continues, Bordwell misses the fact that the "young angst" the director clearly revels in can stand for the love, loss, and emotional pain anyone at any age might experience. Is it not an unfair value judgment to denigrate "young angst" in the first place? I suspect that this emotion, and the delicious frisson that it can activate, looks quite different to a young person than to someone middle-aged, and neither response can be considered correct or normative. Furthermore, in the context of the commercial cinema that Bordwell privileges in his groundbreaking book on the Hong Kong film industry, it is clear that, given the film's origin as a vehicle for Andy Lau, Wong would have had no choice, in this first film, but to focus on glamorous young people even had he desired to do otherwise. In any case, through this reasoning, Bordwell is ultimately able to recuperate Wong's cinema for his thesis that genre underlies all: "For all his sophistication, his unembarrassed efforts to capture powerful, pleasantly adolescent feelings confirms his commitment to the popular Hong Kong tradition" (*Planet* 281).

Interestingly, though he seems vaguely to disapprove, Bordwell provides a succinct and useful expression of the ways in which Wong differs from his Hong Kong colleagues, if ever so tentatively, in *As Tears Go By:* "Wong stands out from his peers by abandoning the kinetics of comedies and action movies in favor of more liquid atmospherics. He dissolves crisp emotions into vaporous moods" (281). It is precisely this feature of Wong's work—this productive clash of cultures and aesthetics, which some critics have censured as "Europeanization"—that makes him such a provocative filmmaker. It is, after all, the hybrid that fascinates.

The "liquid atmospherics" are what Wong's cinema, at least formally speaking, is all about. Ungerböck, an experienced observer of Asian cinema, has claimed that the visual style displayed in *As Tears Go By* was truly new and was copied all over Asia in television and film. This popularity led quickly to Wong's being acclaimed as a cult director (26). Despite Ungerböck's insistence on Wong's novelty, though, the film's visual regime—bright primary colors and unnatural hues shot from bizarre camera angles and juxtaposed through jumpy editing—may be partially a legacy of the quasi-experimental filmmaker Patrick Tam, with whom Wong worked, especially on *Final Victory* (1987), his best film. According to the critic Stephen Teo, the visual structure of all of Tam's films—which Teo doesn't really approve of, because of what he sees as their excessive formalism—is based on the coordination of primary colors (156). Tam may thus be the principal source of this technique that was to be heavily used, in a more radicalized form, in *As Tears Go By* and Wong's subsequent films.

Even the opening credit sequence of *As Tears Go By* bears out this interest in juxtaposing extremes in color, as the credits are inscribed on the far left of the screen in shouting reds (the text) and yellows (the neon lights behind). The largest part of the screen, however, is occupied by a severely angled bank of television sets that, plunging diagonally toward the center, display the bright blue of the sky and clouds that pass by on the multiple screens, in a fashion reminiscent of the work of the video artist Nam June Paik. This intensely saturated visual field will be echoed throughout the film by the omnipresent, garish colors of the various neon signs associated with different night spots, especially the Future club, on whose logo the colors and direction of the opening image have been reversed. Beyond this, though, Wong relies throughout on a deep blue image that signifies nighttime rather than the traditional black (or however "black" has been conventionally suggested by sculpting with various amounts of light); the effect is to signify time in quasi-conventional terms while also loading it expressively.

Curtis K. Tsui goes beyond an expressive reading of this binary opposition of colors to develop a specific and plausible interpretation that ties it more closely to the narrative. He argues that the credit sequence displays the film's two opposing "'spaces' of radically different tone and emotion," different spaces that will come to be associated with Ngor and Fly: "The blue skies and white clouds that appear on the TV screens suggest one of idyllic calm, whereas the darkened streets imply one of more somber proportions" (97). Even more intriguing is his suggestion that the film's Chinese title, *Mongkok Carmen,* which juxtaposes the brutal reality of a rough section of Hong Kong with the promise of love found in Bizet's opera, participates in this binary as well. For Tsui, these are the first signs of a specific political thematic—one that I will address more fully later—that operates throughout the film and that transcends character.

In another, somewhat overheated but provocative reading of this same juxtaposition found in the opening credits, which deserves to be quoted at length, the French critic Ackbar Abbas claims that it represents the clash between the slower, older world of material objects found in emporiums, and the dematerialized, placeless and instantly commutable space of the televisual. . . . It is not a question of rapid change and metamorphosis—a commonplace theme—but rather of anamorphosis, of how the historical grids by which we understand the image have themselves undergone change without our noticing. . . . We never find synesthesias, but always disjunction, dissemination, fugue. This results in a characteristic effect: in Wong's cinema, we are never certain about what we are seeing. The image always subtly misses its mark. (44–45)

Abbas is right that this "missing" that occurs in visual representation is an important thematic nexus in many of Wong's films, but it appears at most in only embryonic form in his debut film.

Once the film proper begins, the first thing we see is an overhead shot of a sleeping figure, marked by strong lines of bright color, neatly slicing the bed in two, which produces an almost chiaroscuro effect. As in the credit sequence, we are being signaled that a large part of this film's drama will be visual in nature. And not only in the sense that dramatic scenes will be visualized for us—the nature of the graphic image itself, the organization of shape, color, and line, will be the site of much of the film's emotional "conflict," conceived in the broadest sense. Nor, the film suggests, will the classic Aristotelian unity of place be respected, as we see a cutaway (or several)[2] of Wah's cousin Ngor, who is about to visit him in Mongkok, on the boat. The shots or shot, which seem produced directly from Wah's consciousness, appear to be overtly "composed" in a classically aesthetic manner. Here and elsewhere the director seems completely uninterested in any documentarylike, handheld Barthesian "effect of the real." The contrast between Wah's everyday, violent world and the possibilities of release and redemption represented by his cousin Ngor, rhyming with the binary of the opening credits, is figured visually from the opening images of the film, even before the narrative has begun.

Because it is such a perfect "picture-postcard moment," however, replete with an artfully arranged sunset, it's difficult to know exactly how serious Wong is being here. In other words, is this film to be simply a clichéd romantic story, fleshed out by pretty pictures? This alternative, at least in any strict sense, seems doubtful. Or is it a clichéd romantic story redeemed (that is, made postmodern) by irony and self-awareness of its clichés? This purposely conflicted, self-conscious ambiguity is continued in the first shots of Ngor after she has gotten to Wong's apartment, when this beautiful woman—the recently crowned Miss Hong Kong who will go on to become the celebrated, ravishing movie star Maggie Cheung[3]—wears, owing to the possibility of an unspecified pulmonary disease, a highly unromantic gauze mask over her mouth. In counterpoint, the dreamy music on the sound track cues us to the amorous potential of this unlikely but clearly foreordained couple. Even the nature of her possible illness—an unknown lung ailment that makes her cough picturesquely—points self-consciously to Mimi (*La Bohéme*), Marguérite Gauthier (*La Traviata*), and a host of other romantic operatic heroines, who in turn recall the Carmen of the film's Chinese title. What's most interesting here is that an unlovely and jarring visual cue—which has special if unforeseen resonance in our own SARS-threatened world—contradicts or troubles the expected romantic aural cue.

Wong's camera offers a continuously surprising sense of play throughout, which will become his visual signature, and the viewer never knows what is going to come next. All of this seems substantially different from most other Hong Kong films, which, though themselves different from Hollywood movies, tend to be different in different ways than Wong's films are. His cuts are sudden and unmotivated, time disappears like it's been vacuumed out of the frame, and all extraneous narrative information is rigorously suppressed. A given sequence—say, a character moving from one side of the room to another—may be relayed through a series of quick cuts from a variety of different angles, shots that are, strictly speaking, narratively and cognitively unnecessary and seem to be retained primarily for expressive purposes. Then, for example, we cut to a dramatic, mysterious extreme close-up of the end of a cigarette being lit, a shot that in its disproportionate scale reminds one of Charlie's suddenly gigantic finger in Truffaut's *Shoot the Piano Player,* or Michel's huge revolver in Godard's *Breathless.* The exhaled smoke creates an expressive blue shape that an initially unknown, dark figure enters, to approach a glowing TV screen, which gives off its own suggestive visual feel. At this point we realize that the camera is contortionistically shooting Wah from a position exactly below, rhyming the overhead shot with

which the film began. (Similarly, in a later shot on Ngor's face, we see her, against all expectations, upside-down.)

Now that the soft side of Wah has been established (though not without a series of hints that there's more to him than this), and the audience's identification with him is secured, we move to the polar opposite of this initial encounter with the romantic possibility of escape to discover the underground world in which our hero is deeply mired, the nasty and uncompromising world of the triads. In retrospect we can see how clever Wong was to present Wah first as a benign, even appealing romantic figure. Now we see him in his other persona, that of a brutally violent gangster who abjures talking for the raw certainty of direct action.

Once Wah moves to the Future nightclub (significantly named, perhaps, since his future is what is in play here), he pushes his girlfriend Mabel around after she reveals she's had an abortion. She is dressed in a startling red dress that is set off by her red, red lips; both contrast with the blue of the surrounding atmosphere of the nightclub. The aural track is equally hyperactive here and elsewhere, with a jangling phone, for example, offering a cacophony that sets the emotional and psychological context for more than one scene.

Later, when he returns to his apartment, Wah tries to smash everything in it, a gesture performed by Kane in Welles's film and by countless other cinematic male protagonists disappointed in love and life. (In a wonderful example of the notorious Hong Kong penchant for inadvertently silly subtitles, his cousin Ngor innocently asks him, "Are you lovelorned?") Soon after, there is a resonant shot of him bathed in blue light, contrasted with her in natural light. The meaning here is in some sense specifically symbolic—and it's not difficult to figure out—but, as in the films of Antonioni, it's also meant in a more generally expressive way, conveying something of their different worlds in abstract, never precisely specifiable terms.

The next morning, they eat together, consuming food that Ngor has prepared. Thus begins Wong's motif of the interrelation of food and love, a theme that will reappear throughout his career and will come to its full flowering in *In the Mood for Love*. Here, as in the later film, the camera is precisely balanced between the two figures, as they are pinned against the flat background, specimens being subjected to

Wong's almost clinical gaze. The long-held, utterly static shot serves as a contrast to everything visual that has gone before.

For pure kinetic action, the scene of retributive violence that follows soon after simply can't be beaten. Fly, Wah's "little brother" or protégé, has antagonized a fellow gangster in a pool hall and gotten beaten up in the process. Wah must avenge this humiliation, which affects his status in the gangster hierarchy as much as it affects Fly physically. The staging and spectacularization of Wah's righteous wrath are brilliantly realized, and it becomes clear that if Wong had chosen to follow a purely generic route in his career, he could have done very well indeed. The scene begins with a dissolve to a close-up of Wah's face, bathed in blue light, which is superimposed over a foggy red background, thus restating the film's basic color scheme. (In the restaurant, the basic blue coloration is disturbed for a second by an anonymous woman's washed-out red dress, creating an otherworldly emphatic effect similar to that of the little girl singled out in Spielberg's *Schindler's List.*) The resolute look on Wah's face, accompanied by martial music, is calculated to thrill the audience, no matter how much doubt Wong elsewhere in the film casts upon the macho code the gangsters religiously adhere to. Slow motion is heavily used for the first time, as the two antagonists are placed on an irreconcilable collision course. To prepare us emotionally, Wong first shows the bad guy manhandling a cat. The gesture is obviously manipulative, yet it's so blatant that it seems meant as part of the arch generic fun. (In a similar vein, there is a self-reflexive, jokey quality to some of the film's images, a playfulness that will disappear in Wong's later films. For example, at one point there is a quick cut to the gangsters. First, the two thugs on the far left and far right jump up, then the two on each side closer in, then the leader in the middle, a choreographed series that results in a sudden, comical breaking of the realistic illusion.)

A series of wild cuts follows in the fight scene, and, purposely it seems, we have little idea of who is doing what to whom. While the emotional logic of the scene has set us up to associate the origin of the mayhem with Wah, the nearly sanctified aggressor, we seem meant to react primarily to the violence in a removed, abstract way rather than to take the side of one character over another. As in many Hong Kong genre films, the violence itself provides the excitement, rather than any narrow psychological identification with a specific character. At one point, though, we do focus on Wah, as we witness the drama of a single line of blood streaming down his face. In this way, the color scheme becomes as emotionally charged as the film speed in the way it works on us, and the combination of the two is powerful.

Tsui sees what he calls the "stop-action style" of this and other violent or passionate scenes as being "representative of temporal and spatial incoherence" (98), but this description, which he never elaborates upon, is vague and unsatisfactory. (In fact, Wong's visual technique here has important implications for his attempt to reconfigure the relation between space and time. But since this effect is more evident in subsequent films, I will postpone a more detailed discussion until later.) Bordwell, characteristically careful in his details, explains Wong's innovative slow-motion technique in much more specific and thus more useful technical terms:

> In *As Tears Go By* he devised the technique of shooting action at only eight, ten, or twelve frames per second and then "stretch-printing" the result to the normal twenty-four frames. The comparatively long exposure during filming makes movement blur, while the printing process, repeating each frame two or three times, produces a jerky pulsation. Wong shifts visual accents by using different rates of stretch-printing, adding or deleting frames at different points. (*Planet* 277)

This novel visual wizardry is fully abetted by Wong's fecund aural imagination, which has been at least as well-developed as its visual counterpart from the start of his career, and which works hand in hand with the flamboyant visual track. On a minor scale, what will become Wong's trademark voice-over technique appears in *As Tears Go By*, with Ngor reading letters aloud. (I shall have more to say about this technique with regard to subsequent films, where the device is more clearly foregrounded and more aesthetically significant.) Even more crucial, though, is Wong's superb use of music, a resource that will grow in significance and power with each succeeding film. It is notoriously difficult to talk about a musical score, but in this film, it is chiefly memorable for its heavy yet subtly complex discordance during Wah's violent encounters with his many adversaries.

Much more aurally important in this film is Wong's use of the internationally successful pop tune "Take My Breath Away"—translated here, except for the title line, into Chinese—which dominates the last part of the movie. Bordwell has written approvingly of the way that Wong uses songs as "part of the expressive atmosphere bathing his characters" and especially commends the complexity of his approach. His trenchant observations are worth quoting in full:

> Consider the "Take My Breath Away" music montage in *As Tears Go By*. Wah pursues Ngor, then he leaves her, and then she races to catch up with him. Wong introduces a series of devices one by one—rhythmic cutting, figure movement paced to the beat, bursts of color (an orange-and-yellow bus shearing across the image), conflicting lateral movements throughout the frame, and stretch-printing when Wah springs into the shot, grabs Ngor, and jogs her into the bus shelter for some desperate kissing. Wong caps it by slowly scalding color out of the image as the couple clutch each other. Unlike most music videos, this sequence holds each image long enough to permit expressive elements to accumulate and step up the lyrical intensity. It is flashy and ingratiating but also rigorous. (*Planet* 279)

It might also be added that this wordless, silent scene (silent apart from the self-consciously rapturous "Take My Breath Away") is the most powerful, emotionally convincing one in the entire film.

While we have thus far been concerned with the generic and formal, expressionistic elements of the film, which to my mind are its salient features, character and theme, though less fully developed, need to be considered as well. Wah is the traditional figure of the tough guy with a heart of gold, a figure that goes back at least as far as Humphrey Bogart. But he's younger than Bogart, and what makes him even more attractive for Wong's original target audience is that he's a stark representative of "troubled youth" as well. Beyond the acceptance of Wah's tragic dilemma (the demands of honor and friendship versus personal salvation through love), Wong's script spends virtually no time tracing Wah's underworld connections, and no sociological theories are advanced to explain his sociopathy. He is merely accepted for what and how he is, which is, of course, fully in keeping with generic expectations. As always, audience identification with such an ambivalent and conflicted character must be delicately managed, and thus when he manhandles his pregnant girlfriend, it's never violently enough to turn us against him.

In an interview with Tony Rayns seven years after the film was released, Wong said, "I'm still trying to understand the character played by Andy Lau in *As Tears Go By*. He's a gangster, and I don't know what he thinks or what motivates him. The other characters are easy to understand: I know exactly what the cousin [Ngor] and the impulsive kid [Fly] are thinking. But not him. My curiosity about this character carried over in to the characters played by Leslie Cheung in *Days of Being Wild* and *Ashes of Time*" (Rayns, "Poet" 14). Wong indicated in another interview that Wah's indefiniteness is what defines him: "All through the making of *As Tears Go By* I had no clue what Andy Lau's role was after—What did he want? Was he tired of the triad life, or was the girl just a passing stage for him? All of this, I cannot answer. But now, of course, I can say that there are people who are like that, having no clear idea what they themselves want, just drifting about" (Ngai 105).

The film's subsidiary characters are, in a way, actually much more interesting and complex than Wah. Ngor points forward toward the central situation of Wong's subsequent films, the eternal impossibility of love. Here, however, constraining outside circumstances limit one's chances for emotional happiness, whereas in later films the inherent contradictions of love itself will be to blame. Fly is motivated in more complicated ways than Wah, since all of Fly's impulsive, self-destructive choices are seen as emanating from an existential desire, present since childhood, to make his mark in the world. For him, success is solely a function of his status within the world of the triads, which is, in turn, a function of how much money he has. He knows he must die to ensure that his life has been meaningful, and he willingly embraces his fate; Wah, on the contrary, seems more a victim to abstract principles, reluctantly embraced, than anything else. In a classic scene with a modest Shakespearean resonance, Fly rejects Wah's friendship in order to save him, but to no avail.

Is there more in this debut film? Beyond its lightly sketched character motivations, does it have a meaning that transcends the immediate stimulation of the simple story and the visual and aural sensation? For Tsui, the contradictory joining of love and violence in one person, Wah, is symbolic of the contradictions in Hong Kong society itself. He sees the film as "Wong's allegorical representation of a Hong Kong in search of its culture and identity" (100), but his attempt to locate this dynamic in the binary of the two plots isn't convincing. Tsui further claims that the negativity in the film (Fly's fatalistic behavior, Wah's choice of Fly over Ngor) is related to the looming handover of Hong Kong by the British authorities to the Chinese government set to take place nine years in the future: "Wong's feelings regarding Hong Kong's search for its sense of self appear somewhat pessimistic within *As Tears Go By*. There is an almost palpable sense of impending doom and loss that pervades the movie, evocative of the city's nearing future" (100). While these remarks are provocative and not to be excluded by any means (especially since the political theme is evident in some of Wong's later films), nevertheless they feel forced and extraneous to the experience of watching this particular film. Tsui's close readings of other images in the film, especially the final ones, which he links to specific political events in the British colony, are seriously overblown.

We will do better, I think, to turn to the perspicacious Ackbar Abbas for a more philosophical and yet perhaps more modest summation of the film's relation to Hong Kong's political situation. Like Tsui, he is taken by the film's negativity, which he describes as being "related to the problematic nature of a colonial space making the transition from imperialism to multinational capitalism, a space where all the rules have quietly changed. In the film itself, however, the political implications of negativity are expressed only indirectly, in the characters' futile attempt to live their lives in the negativity of the city, which ultimately destroys them" (53).

One final relevant point regarding the status of this film should be mentioned. *As Tears Go By* is also interesting, in a more minor sense, because it provides an answer to a question that has animated debates regarding Wong's status as an auteur since the beginning. Since all of his films after this auspicious debut have been photographed by Christopher Doyle, with set design by William Chang, some critics have suggested that Doyle and Chang are at least as responsible as Wong for the unique look that has come to be associated with his films, and even for their artistic success. While auteurist debates of this sort are usually a waste of time, nevertheless it seems clear that while Wong was more or less on his own in *As Tears Go By*, much of what has come to be associated with his filmmaking can already be found here in embryo. Chang and Doyle, in other words, have only enhanced what was already there.

Some further, more negative evidence can also be gleaned from Doyle's own foray into directing, the almost unwatchable *Away with Words* (1999). This failed film makes it clear that innovative cinematography alone is never enough and that it can lead to empty formalist exercises without a narrative, themes, and complex characters to anchor it. Doyle himself said in a 1997 French interview that "Wong Kar-wai's great quality is that he's calm. He knows how to step back, get some distance, be objective. I've got my head stuck into it, I'm not a director, I don't have the perception and distance that he does. All the great directors have that objectivity in regard to things, even the most passionate. Each time, Wong looks for a better solution, a better image, a more interesting way to do the scene" (Niogret, "Entretien" 17).

Reaction to *As Tears Go By* when it first appeared was mixed. It didn't do well commercially in Hong Kong, but its tremendous success in Korea and Taiwan led to its eventually garnering nine Hong Kong Oscar nominations. And lest those devoted (and nearly always insightful) Wong supporters at *Positif* think that they have supported the director's films from the start, their brief review of this first effort dismissed it as resembling "the most conventional gangster films." Interestingly, the reviewer denigrates the film for *not* being one of the many recent Hong Kong films in which the director was trying to make a personal film while working within the system. And best of all: "All of the technical effects are obviously used to theatricalize violence, to raise it to an operatic level, and to give the film a modish allure which could only fool those who prefer exoticism and hysterical violence, out of ignorance or out of fear of missing the boat" (Niogret, "*As Tears*" 80). I single out *Positif* only because early on, even Wong's subsequently most passionate supporters were fooled by the film's apparent focus on its generic elements. Like many other critics around the world, however, they would soon see the light.

Days of Being Wild

With *Days of Being Wild,* his second film, Wong plunges unequivocally into what will be his greatest themes, love and time, with a *soupçon* of politics added for good measure. At the risk of succumbing to teleo-logical essentialism (which negates history by seeing the future always conveniently and unambiguously prefigured in the past), one could say that from this point on his films become "Wong Kar-wai films." As Tony Rayns puts it, "nothing in Wong's previous work as a screenwriter or director anticipated the structure or poetic density of *Days of Being Wild*" ("Ah Fei" 42).

Based on the unexpected financial and critical success of *As Tears Go By* across Asia, and following the original commercial model established in the earlier film, Wong's producer signed six of the best-known pop singers in Hong Kong for this new venture. Unfortunately, the film—a deliberately paced, experimentally conceived narrative that now looks brilliant—dumbfounded its original audiences. It was, according to Wong, "a complete failure: In Korea, the spectators even threw things at the screen" (Ciment, "Entretien" 42).

Figure 2. *Days of Being Wild*: Yuddy (Leslie Cheung) looks over his latest conquest, Mimi/Lulu (Carina Lau).

As befits Wong's near-total transcendence of genre in this film, its plot is more intricate and emotionally nuanced than that of *As Tears Go By*. Yuddy[4] (played by the late Leslie Cheung, in the first of several stunning appearances in Wong's films) is a strikingly handsome ladies' man who lives with his Aunt Rebecca (Rebecca Pan) and refuses to commit emotionally to either of two successive girlfriends, Su Li-zhen (Maggie Cheung) and Mimi (Carina Lau), who is also called Lulu. Su Li-zhen is quietly loved by a gentle policeman named Tide (Andy Lau), a good listener who tries to help her out of her loneliness and depression after she is rejected by Yuddy. Lulu/Mimi (though she is known at different times as both, neither is her real name) has an admirer as well, Zeb (Jacky Cheung), who is Yuddy's not very dashing best friend. When Auntie finally reveals that Yuddy's real mother, who abandoned him as an infant, lives in the Philippines, he travels there to meet her, but she refuses to see him. Tide, who has since become a sailor, meets Yuddy in a seedy Chinese hotel in the Philippines, where Tide is waiting for his ship. After being rejected by his mother, Yuddy seems to have lost all will to live and comes dangerously close to getting himself and Tide killed in an action-packed imbroglio concerning a fake passport that he doesn't want to pay for. They escape by taking a train, and after a discussion about love and life, during which their earlier connection through Li-zhen is established, Yuddy is killed by gangsters seeking revenge. The final images show a new, unidentified character named Smirk (Tony Leung Chiu-wai) preparing, in an unknown location, to go out for the evening. It is now six years later (one discovers from Wong's remarks in interviews), and Smirk uncannily resembles Yuddy in looks and manner.

The most salient feature of this extraordinary film—obvious even in the plot summary—is the constant, much-remarked theme of the implacable impossibility of love, an emotional nexus that greatly increases in complexity from Wong's previous film. Multiple romantic pairings are suggested, begin to form, and then collapse. Both Li-zhen and Mimi/Lulu want Yuddy, but what Yuddy really wants is his mother. Tide the policeman wants Li-zhen, and Zeb wants Mimi/Lulu. (In *In the Mood for Love*, Wong's masterpiece from 2000, the only natural pair in the film decide voluntarily to keep apart, never consummating their relationship, as though Wong has finally given up altogether on the possibility of love.) Even more tantalizing, perhaps, Rebecca, Yuddy's aging aunt and foster mother, also seems to want Yuddy, since their frustrating and highly charged emotional bonds, based on lies, selfishness, and covert sexual desire, appear at least as complex as the more conventional relationships in the film. (In one scene, responding to Yuddy's objections to her younger gigolo lover, Auntie says, "He makes me happy. Have you?" Later, she provocatively spits out at him, "I want you to hate me. At least that way you won't forget me.") And the chance meeting of Yuddy and Tide in the Philippines hotel near the end of the film has a homoerotic flavor that anticipates Wong's 1997 film *Happy Together*—and recalls the Italian director Luchino Visconti's 1942 film *Ossessione,* where the sublimated "lovers" also discuss their desire to wander the world, perhaps as sailors, in language similar to that of *Days of Being Wild.* Perhaps the only selfless act of love in the entire movie—and, characteristically for Wong, it's an act of renunciation—comes when Zeb gives money to Mimi/Lulu to go to the Philippines in search of Yuddy, from the proceeds of the sale of Yuddy's flashy car, with which Zeb has been entrusted.

While the characters think and talk about love from beginning to end, perversely we never see even a hint of sex on screen. *Days* nevertheless remains ultrasensual, as when Wong invokes decades of steamy-jungle films set in South Asia merely through the noisy blowing of a hyperactive fan. Even a simple cut to a close-up of Auntie invokes a certain sensuality, as for example the insinuating jump from Yuddy lounging suggestively in medium shot to a close-up of Auntie, a cut that implies a certain movement and proximity of bodies, even if it's only a visual effect.

Interlaced with this theme of the hopelessness and perversity of love and desire, or embedded within it, is the relentless passage of time, which is sometimes evoked almost to the point of parody. The loud ticking of a clock during indolent postcoital scenes, for example, is often used as an aural effect, similar to the frequent hammering of the rain. And like the rain, time impinges on the characters and saturates them, almost like an alien force that lays siege from the outside. A cleaning woman ostentatiously cleans a clock, again and again. Auntie visibly ages and incessantly checks her downward progress in a mirror. (All the most selfish characters are narcissistically obsessed with mirrors.) A scene begins with a bizarre, angled close-up on Zeb's wristwatch. As in many Wong films to come, there is constant talk of starting "from this minute" or, "let's remember this very moment." (Yuddy's initial come-on line to Li-zhen concerns the precise time when they first speak—one minute before 3:00 P.M. on April 16, 1960—which becomes a running motif in the film.) At another point, Li-zhen refers to the subjective nature of time: "I always think a minute can pass fast, but sometimes it takes long." Later, in an antirealist sequence, the camera tracks quickly to a large clock, we hear a loud gong, and the big gate of the stadium in which Li-zhen works is suddenly shut. In the Philippines hotel room, Yuddy asks Tide what time it is, because his watch has been stolen. This unceasing desire to capture the present moment, for whatever reason, is always defeated, as the present is always already gone as soon as we begin to look for it.

In his remarks about the film, Wong seems intensely aware of the passing of his own youth, which is perhaps a chief psychological motivation for the film's fascinating exploration of temporality. He told Michel Ciment that he was acutely conscious of having turned thirty when he came to make this film, which is set in the 1960s, shortly after Wong's arrival in the colony from Shanghai at age five. More than anything, he said, "I wanted to evoke the things that I was afraid of forgetting later" (Ciment, "Entretien" 42).

Wong says that he originally wanted to set the film in 1963, when he came to Hong Kong as a five-year-old, but moved it back to 1960 because of the election of John F. Kennedy (as he says in one interview) or the Apollo space mission (as he says in another). In any case, "there was a sense that we were moving into a new page of history. . . . Since I didn't have the resources to re-create the period realistically, I decided to work entirely from memory. And memory is actually about a sense of loss—always a very important element in drama. We remember things in terms of time: 'Last night I met. . . .' 'Three years ago, I was. . . .'" (Rayns, "Poet" 14). More explicitly, he told Bérénice Reynaud that "the Hong Kong of *Days of Being Wild* is set in the sixties, but the society as shown in the film never really existed like that, it's an invented world, an imaginary past" ("Entretien" 39). Memory and time thus become intertwined here, as, of course, they always are. Interestingly, the end of the film is set in 1966, six years after its principal events—at least this is the way Wong describes it, since there is no actual time marker

in the film itself—which is when a projected second part, never made, was to have begun.

Wong's concern with time is also formally echoed in the film's tempo, which alternates dramatically between long moments of stasis and sudden, powerful outbreaks of violent movement. This tempo is also manifested in the alteration between very tight shots and extreme long shots, both of which seem primarily expressive rather than narrative in intent. As further evidence of the rigorous calculation of Wong's approach, which may superficially seem rather helter-skelter, he described the film as having

> a rather slow tempo that corresponded with my idea of the sixties. I tried to divide the film into four movements. The first was very Bressonian, with lots of close-ups. The second had the look of a B movie, with very complicated camera movements and long takes. The third was filmed in deep focus. The fourth looked more like the second, with lots of mobility. The story moved equally from one character to the other, which made the different movements more visible. (Ciment, "Entretien" 42)

This elaborate system (whose accuracy is borne out by close examination) was apparently meant to serve as structure for the film, supplementing the langorously paced, uneventful narrative that must have baffled its original audience, expecting, as they were, to see their favorite stars *doing things,* performing, rather than just standing around talking. But apart from the rigorous aesthetic schema of the film, what keeps a viewer involved? Is it the cool attractiveness of the characters? This is certainly a factor in our fascination with Yuddy. Zeb confesses to Mimi/Lulu that though Yuddy has given him his car, it's hopeless because he'll never be able to "match" his friend behind the wheel because he is just too cool. So part of the film's attraction obviously lies in its devotion to "cool" or to style. Yet it also seems clear that along with indulging it, at some level Wong is probing this stance as well, suggesting that, like the superficially exciting macho code of honor in *As Tears Go By,* it gets in the way of authentic human encounters.

Everything in this film, however, eventually comes back to the confluence of love and time. In a reversal of Henry James's classic dictum to show rather than tell, "we have had the narrating of the love story instead of the story itself," as Larry Gross succinctly describes the affair between Yuddy and Lu-zhin. "We have seen the characters project into the future and reflect on the past as if the present is too fragile to be directly represented. Narration, here as elsewhere, has performed a strange surgical incision into different fragments of time" (9).

The theme of time also goes beyond its ageless philosophical expression, for as in any Hong Kong movie of artistic ambition made during this period, time also has a political dimension. In 1984, mainland Chinese and British authorities agreed to the handover of Hong Kong to the People's Republic in 1997. Hence, the ticking clock, in Wong's films and the films of other directors, became a natural metaphor for all the fear and anxiety attached to this change. As Stephen Teo puts it, the clock in this film "is an obvious allusion to the 1997 syndrome yet again" (195). Carbon even goes so far as to claim that the film was a commercial failure precisely because Wong insisted on talking about memory, "a taboo subject in a city without past or future" (37).

In any case, from various comments Wong has made, it is clear that this political dimension was in his mind from the beginning, though in more nebulous terms than those proposed by many critics. Wong seems to have been vaguely interested in linking the present with the past, and geography with history. The director told Tony Rayns that "*Days* centers on various feelings about staying in or leaving Hong Kong. . . . I tried to evoke two different families from the first postwar generation. One is Cantonese and is originally from Hong Kong, and the other, Leslie Cheung's [Yuddy's], comes from Shanghai. They're separated by language, and in the second part [never filmed] they end up getting to know each other" ("Poet" 14). Expanding a bit, he told Reynaud that Yuddy is Filipino, his stepmother is from Shanghai, and Tide is from Hong Kong. "The character played by Maggie Cheung is in between since she is from Macao. I wanted to see how they would interact, since, in the 1960s, it was still rare to see Hong Kong natives and immigrants mix" (Reynaud, "Entretien" 37). In any case, if Stephen Teo's interpretation of the film's sociopolitical aspect is perhaps a little too schematic—he says that the film presents "lost youths as an allegory for the plight of Hong Kong's people as they prepare for the transition to 1997" (193)—it's nevertheless clear that the characters *are* historically determined and not only representative of some putative general 1960s decadence. (In this regard, Wong's films are similar to Antonioni's in their mix of aesthetics and politics.)

If the characters are historically determined, they are also curiously intertwined through repetition. Ackbar Abbas has said that "instead of linear plots, then, what we now find is a serial structure of repetition. Most of the film is taken up with permutating the sets of possible relations among the six main characters, in a series of affective tableaux" (55).[5] Repetition does indeed abound. At the end, six years later, the barely glimpsed Smirk repeats Yuddy's familiar hair-combing gesture, suggesting that he will be taking over for the dead Yuddy where he left off. Mimi and Yuddy share a strange narcissism, even when they're apart, dancing lasciviously, and alone, before the camera, in front of mirrors, everywhere, in that 1960s swaying gesture that follows the Hawaiian-guitar music on the sound track. Mimi also has three names with which she identifies herself to different people, as though consciously repeating herself. Like the binary opposition between Yuddy (romantic) and Tide the policeman (practical realist), which is always also a kind of repetition, Mimi is clearly paired with Su Li-zhen as her double and polar opposite (sexy good-time girl versus plain beauty, Violet versus Mary in Capra's *It's a Wonderful Life*, Chihuahua versus Clementine in Ford's *My Darling Clementine*), even down to their carefully articulated differences in body language.

One aspect of this repetitiveness is that, like Hong Kong itself, the characters of *Days* share a common search for their identity. This ancient theme, which goes back at least to Homer's *Odyssey,* is brought up to date by Wong. Mimi has at least three names. Tide restlessly wanders the globe after his mother's death frees him to be a sailor. To achieve psychological integrity, Li-zhen must establish herself as separate from Yuddy. Yuddy himself is the figure most conspicuously looking for an identity. The orb around which this entire constellation revolves,[6] he is a thoroughgoing romantic, yet he has an ugly streak of violence in him that is reminiscent of Ah Wah from *As Tears Go By,* as when he beats up Auntie's gigolo lover early in the film. His way of being in the world is primarily that of a heartless seducer, but what motivates his most decisive actions is his desire to know his mother, and thus his origins. When Auntie finally reveals his mother's identity and he goes to find her in the Philippines, we share his crushing disappointment at not being able to meet with her. This calamitous nonencounter, so crucial for Yuddy's fate, is dramatically underlined (and consequently stylized) principally because it is the only time in the film that slow-motion is used. Since his mother has denied him the possibility of seeing her, he tells us in voiceover, he refuses to look back in order to deny her the chance to see his face surreptitiously from behind her curtains. Since this too is a moment of unrequited love, the Hawaiian-guitar theme that marks moments throughout the film when sexual love is frustrated is heard here as well.

Yet if we are invited to share Yuddy's individual consciousness and inner search, the film's title also suggests that he is a specific type. The "A Fei" of the Chinese title *A Fei Zhengzuan,* according to Stephen Teo, is a phrase that was a "common euphemism for vaseline-haired and rock-loving delinquents and unsavoury teenagers with gangland connections" (193). Teo points out that Yuddy is "A Fei" but vulnerable too, and in that combination he reminds us of James Dean in *Rebel without a Cause* (194). Bordwell also helpfully points out that the Cantonese title, translated literally into English, is "The Story of Rebellious Youth," the same title that *Rebel without a Cause* is known by in Hong Kong (*Planet* 38).

The richness of the film's political and psychological themes is well supported technically. Camera angles, camera movement, and framing are especially noteworthy and often brilliantly expressive. Relentless close-ups on Yuddy and Li-zhen mark the first, claustrophobic part of the film, precisely as Wong described it in the interview quoted earlier. In addition, there are many scenes throughout in which a character nearest to the camera is in focus while another, further back, is completely out of focus. It is interesting that this choice seems never to be based on which character is delivering the dialogue at the moment but rather on the possibility of maximum visual expressivity of the character facing the camera. There are also long sequences in which Wong refuses the conventional shot/reverse shot alternation in favor of keeping the camera on only one of the characters—despite the fact that the character is engaged in a two-way conversation—presumably, once again, to remain focused on facial expression.

At least twice during the film there are moments that recall the camera placement of the Japanese master Yasujiro Ozu, as for example when characters stare straight into the camera, breaking whatever realist illusion has been established up to that point. Thus when Yuddy is leaving for the Philippines, he opens some French doors and seems to stare straight at us. We then hear a foghorn (unjustified by anything visible in the frame or narratively in the setting) that, in a highly stylized manner, suggests his impending trip. He then vacates the frame, though Wong holds the shot another ten seconds on the empty interior. At that point we cut frontally to Auntie, who looks provocatively over her shoulder back at him (and us), directly into the camera from within an entirely artificial space. (Differently from Ozu, however, Wong tends to position his camera higher, just above his characters' heads, shooting slightly downward.) It is as though Wong becomes impatient with the generally realistic texture of the film at such moments and allows himself a brief outbreak of stylized expression. Consistently undercut as it is, however, the film's apparent realism is never more than apparent; the many interiors are glimpsed only fragmentarily, behind character close-ups, and are never even visually, let alone spatially, explored. Even the *exterior* shots focus almost exclusively on characters, usually seen only in close-up or in stylized long shots, and blot out any contextualizing reality to the extent that they end up feeling even more (purposely) artificial than the interiors. This technique will reach its zenith in Wong's 1997 film, *Happy Together.*

Yet the camera is always actively looking, even if only at the characters or at their absence, as it were. For example, after Yuddy has left the room in the scene described above, or when Zeb presents Lulu with the money for her trip to the Philippines in the restaurant booth, the camera remains for a disconcertingly long time on his empty place after he leaves. That looking is important can be seen in Yuddy's refusal of his mother's gaze in the Philippines and, earlier in the film, when Lulu is staring at Yuddy and Auntie in Queen's Cafe, playfully looking around a match box. And virtually no one can pass a mirror without preening; Wong often chooses to view characters through their mirror reflections, further underlining the subjective nature of all that we see and implicating our own (and the director's) looking in the process.

The most powerful camera movement in *Days of Being Wild*—powerful precisely because it stands in such contrast to its usually stationary role in the film—comes with a Steadicam shot that races across the square and up the stairs to the restaurant on top of the train station when, near the end of the film, Yuddy goes to pick up his fake passport. As though finally released from the restraint of being shackled to the characters, the dynamic camera flies through space untied to any specific individual. Then, when Yuddy stabs the man who has provided the passport, the film's inherent generic longings, as it were, also seem to break free in a wild melee of kung fu, though the fisticuffs last only a minute or two, almost as though Wong is making fun of the pleasure we take in this tiny bit of kinetic activity and generic frivolity he gratuitously tosses our way after such a long period of stasis.

Much of the visual effect of the film comes through its lighting, or better, its lack of it. An amazing amount of time is spent in the dark or in the rain, or both, which leads to a slow, stylized expressivity—similar to later films like *Happy Together* and *In the Mood for Love*—that never contains more than a modicum of narrative information and perfectly matches the mood of the rest of the film. Contrasting moments of intense light, as when Yuddy visits his mother's palatial estate in the Philippines, are very powerful and seem to betoken an unreal world beyond the grasp of the characters and perhaps beyond our ken as well, since we have learned in this film that the real world is nearly always murky and difficult to decipher (a knowledge abetted by all the mirror shots that remove us even further from a direct perception of "reality").

Regarding the lighting, Wong has said that "*Days of Being Wild* was a reaction against my first film, *As Tears Go By*, which was full of harsh light and neon. I told Chris [Doyle, his cinematographer and cameraman] I wanted to do a 'monochrome' film, almost drained of colour. It's a film about different kinds of depression, and it needed to be very blank, very thin in texture. That created many problems for Chris: many filters, few lights, very hard to control focus. That's one reason it took so long to shoot" (Rayns, "Poet" 13). Wong explained to Andreas Ungerböck that he originally wanted to make the film in black and white, but the producer wouldn't let him. He wanted "the light to be very weak, without contrast, as in the paintings of Edward Hopper. I didn't want the light to disturb or to be too obtrusive" (27).

Beyond the stunning visuals, much of what is powerful in the film, as always, comes from Wong's brilliant handling of sound, especially music, a talent that was soon to become his trademark. Here the film is bound together by the late 1950s–style romantic Hawaiian guitar music that begins and ends it and that regularly pops up in between, along with other lushly orchestrated music of the period. What is created is thus an authentic sense of contemporary popular culture that adds to the film's presentation of the psychological texture of its historical setting, as well as an unconventional universe of sound of a sort rarely heard in film.

Wong's mastery of sound extends to the poetic voice-overs as well, which's, somewhat bizarrely, spoken by more than one of the film's characters. Rather than fragmenting the film's effect, however, they connect these otherwise disparate figures while articulating the film's themes. As David Bordwell has put it, "the monologues are purely confessional, issuing from some parallel realm, pouring out across sequences to create links and symmetries, recollections and prefigurations" (*Planet* 275). Teo has even said that these voice-overs, which he calls "mind-dialogues," make *Days of Being Wild* "possibly the most literary of Hong Kong films" (194). He likens the technique to that of Joseph L. Mankiewicz in films like *All About Eve*.

It is here that the film's principal poetic effect resides, especially in the repeated, in principle very "uncinematic" (because literary) use of the self-consciously mythic bird motif that helps to structure the narrative. Yuddy, ever the romantic, tells us early in the film of a mythical bird who never stops flying because it has no legs. It sleeps while it flies, and it only stops once, when it dies. Clearly, he is describing his own situation, and in the most romantic terms possible.[7] At the end of the film, however, Tide, the clear-eyed former policeman who comes from a poor family, interrupts Yuddy with a surprisingly complete knowledge of the myth after Yuddy has barely begun to recount it. The effect is to demean the tale, mythmaking in general, and, more specifically, Yuddy's dangerous romantic approach to life. Tide cynically asks Yuddy, "Are you a bird? If you could fly you wouldn't be here." Tide also brutally insists that given the way Yuddy treated his two girlfriends, he is nothing more than "garbage picked up in Chinatown." Once Yuddy is dead, the truth, now articulated in voice-over by Tide, becomes clear: the bird has always already been dead.

The finale of the movie oozes romanticism, but again, as with *As Tears Go By*, it's difficult to say how much Wong is indulging it and how much he is critiquing this sometimes irresponsible attitude toward life. As with his ambivalent use of the bird myth, it is probably equal parts of both. In any case, the film's themes are intricately and poetically expressed in its last ten minutes, and it may be useful, in order to understand Wong's method of complexly juxtaposing a variety of images and sounds, to examine these final scenes more closely.

After Tide shoots most of the gangsters while rescuing Yuddy in the restaurant, they escape along the top of a corrugated metal roof, which is presumably the train station (we hear the whistle of a train). We cut to an overhead light that is blinking on and off and then to an overhead shot of them lounging in their respective seats on the train. Yuddy tries to engage Tide in inconsequential talk, but Tide is still upset by their brush with death and castigates Yuddy for his irresponsibility. Yuddy responds with a general expression of the transience and unpredictability of life, but Tide will have none of it and brutally punctures Yuddy's comforting bird myth before going off to find out how much longer their trip will be. While he is speaking to the conductor, a man in a white shirt passes him.

We then cut to a subjective shot of an unknown person stumbling down the car toward a sleeping Yuddy. It is the man in the white shirt, whom we see only for a second as he shoots Yuddy point-blank. Tide walks back and discovers an apparently dead Yuddy. Then we cut suddenly to a well-dressed woman walking around the oculus of an exclusive-looking, columned hospital. The camera circles around her in a long arc and, as it looks down through the hole of the oculus onto the lower floor, we see Auntie being handed a baby. Her voiceover tells us how happy she is because she is finally free, since she will now get fifty dollars per month until the boy is eighteen. We thus come to understand what her primary interest in Yuddy has been all along, and Wong may be offering this scene—and the lack of love it implies—as an indirect explanation for Yuddy's treatment of Li-zhen and Mimi and ultimately for his death. We cut back to a close-up in the train car on a sweaty-faced, dying Yuddy (though it may also be merely a flashback). He says that he will not close his eyes when he dies because he wants to know the final thing he sees. When he asks Tide what he wants to see when he dies, Tide replies, "Life is so long, and I have not yet seen many things." Yuddy responds, "Life is actually not so long." Then a shot of a light outside the car. Then back to a dead Yuddy, his eyes wide open, just as he wished. Then we cut to the tracking shot of the mysteriously blue jungle with which the film opened, with the same lush Hawaiian-guitar motif on the sound track. Tide tells us, "There was a bird which flied and flied until it died. It never goes anywhere because it died from the start." He wonders aloud what the woman he will someday love is doing now and comments on the weather. We then see a subjective flashback to the last question Tide asked Yuddy, as a test, about what he was doing at 3:00 P.M. on April 16 last year—the moment that Yuddy and Li-zhen had fetishized—and Yuddy makes it clear that he does indeed remember the girl. "I can remember what should be remembered," he explains, but he instructs Tide to tell Li-zhen that he has forgotten her, since that will be best for all parties concerned. Then, in his present voiceover, Tide wonders if Li-zhen will have forgotten him as well. Cut to Yuddy's dead face, backed up by the lush, romantic music we've heard throughout, followed by an extreme long shot of the speeding train.

At this point, returning to the basic interconnected structural device of the film, the other characters are seamlessly woven back into the narrative. The first one we see is Mimi walking in a colorful outfit along a street in bright sunlight. She has come to the Philippines hotel looking for Yuddy, and though she doesn't find him, her flamboyant dress indicates that she will survive. Then we cut to Li-zhen selling tickets in the bowels of the football stadium where she works and where she first met Yuddy. She seems sad, small, closed-in, again the exact opposite of the vivacious Mimi. In a clear homage to Antonioni's legendary final sequence in *L'eclisse* (1962), Wong cuts to several of the places frequented earlier by Li-zhen and Tide, the lovers who are apparently not to be, but now these places are emptied of all human content except memory. We see where they walked, where the tram tracks come together, and the huge clock behind the grill fence, but not them. Yet we remember. We then cut to Li-zhen reading the paper. She closes her small ticket window (as we hear the sounds of the match in the background), thus making herself disappear. Then we see an extreme long shot of the phone booth (followed by a close shot of the phone), which Tide has earlier told her to call if she ever wanted to talk to him. It rings, but nobody answers.[8] No dialogue, no commentary, no idea of who is calling whom, yet the two shots speak volumes.

Finally we turn to Smirk, the slick gambler played by Tony Leung

Chiu-wai, a completely new character who was to have been the center of the unfilmed second part of the film. It is now 1966, six years after the film begins, and, as Teo has suggested, he's another A Fei, a wild youth. We watch with fascination as he combs his hair in exactly the manner of Yuddy, whom he has in a way become, as he prepares to go out for the night. Again, these preparations are utterly wordless (although we hear the same languorous music on the score that we've heard throughout), as if Wong were suggesting that despite the poetry and truth of the film's multiple voiceovers that have provided a powerful crescendo to the film, real meaning is finally beyond words. It may, however, he seems to suggest, remain obscurely lodged in images and sounds.

Though consistently named by critics as one of the best films ever made in Hong Kong, *Days of Being Wild* was an utter failure at the box office. Incredibly, this seems to have come as a surprise to its director. When asked if he had been prepared for the commercial failure of the film, he replied, "'No, I felt it was going to be a very commercial movie. I thought at that time the gangster movie was approaching a low phase, and there was need for a romantic love story'" (qtd. in Dannen and Long 147).

There is, of course, always a need for a romantic love story, but despite winning five of the awards that are Hong Kong's equivalent to the Oscars, Wong had to return to screenwriting for a number of years before he was able to find the financing for his next project, *Ashes of Time*.

Tony Rayns's succinct summation says it all: "*Days of Being Wild* will remain a peak in [Wong's] filmography, and a landmark in Hong Kong cinema: the first film to rhyme nostalgia for a half-imaginary past with future shock" ("Ah Fei" 42).

Ashes of Time

Ashes of Time represents Wong's second and final foray into genre films, strictly speaking.[9] This time he enters the world of *wuxia* (chivalric warriors practicing the martial arts), a genre that has crossed over into mainstream American movie consciousness by means of Ang Lee's immensely popular *Crouching Tiger, Hidden Dragon* (2000) and is related but not identical to the Hong Kong kung fu film. Predictably, though,

Figure 3. *Ashes of Time*: Murong Yin (Brigitte Lin) asks Ouyang Feng (Leslie Cheung, in background) to kill her brother.

Wong was not content merely to repeat or reinvigorate the genre but decided to reinvent it completely.

What fecundity of imagination—or perversity of artistic willfulness—does it take to shoot a costume epic made up almost entirely of dark rooms, close-ups, and tightly constricted long shots? Or that contains only a handful of repeating, doubled, easily confused characters rather than the proverbial cast of thousands? Or that concerns questions of memory, the past, and emotional isolation rather than honor and the indomitability of the spirit, the themes of the traditional *wuxia* film? Furthermore, where is all the sword fighting that audiences might reasonably have expected to see? While it's true that some stirring action scenes are sprinkled throughout the film, for the most part it's all interiority, longing, and frustration. One dyspeptic observer, Fredric Dannen, called the film one of "the most self-indulgent pictures ever made" (Dannen and Long 51).

Most other critics, including this one, have considered this "self-indulgence" a function of the director's artistic integrity and the film's refusal to be loyal to its genre a very good thing indeed. H. Hampton sees Wong's rejection of generic norms as the most typical and most generic thing about the film: "It's no accident that *Ashes of Time,* an austere, dreamily ironic swordplay epic, is at once so anomalous and so utterly characteristic of Hong Kong film at its most satisfying: where else would someone combine Akira Kurosawa and Alain Resnais to make the equivalent of *The Seven Samurai at Marienbad* (and have this constitute a genre, albeit a genre of one)?" (93).

Wong himself made it clear, in a somewhat testy response to an interviewer, that, despite the time it took to make the film, self-indulgence was the furthest thing from his mind: "The most important thing was the relationship between the characters and the atmosphere created by the film. And there once again I was confronted with the question of time. So it's completely normal that it took me two years to find the maturity to sketch the relations among all these characters. It's a very complex tapestry. I tried a large number of narrative structures and none of them satisfied me. Finally, as my 'sell-by date' approached, I found the solution" (Reynaud, "Entretien" 39).

Set during the Song Dynasty some eight hundred years ago, the film is based loosely on a novel called *Shediao Yingiong Zhuan* (The eagle shooting hero) by the popular writer Jin Yong (also known as Louis Cha), which had been filmed many times previously. Wong has disparaged this novel as a form of "pulp fiction" in comparison with *wuxia* classics like *Novel of the Three Kingdoms* (Ciment, "Entretien" 43). But the modest status of the novel has obviously permitted Wong the luxury of a liberal adaptation, and he has kept barely anything of the original.

What Wong says he especially admired in Jin Yong's work was his ability to mix a fabricated story with real historical events, since the director himself had no interest in ultra-authenticity. "My only criterion was not to mix in elements that came *after* the period of the action, but I decided that objects, clothes, and architectural elements prior to the Song period could be used. I also wanted to avoid slangy, contemporary language, but without consciously seeking an ancient, stylized language either" (Ciment, "Entretien" 44).

The film's Chinese title, *Dongzie Xidu,* translates roughly as "Malevolent East, Malicious West," which are the nicknames of the two heroes,

Huang Yaoshi (Tony Leung Kar-fai, who is Dongzie, or the Malevolent East) and Ouyang Feng (Leslie Cheung, Xidu, or the Malicious West). Wong has said that *Ashes* differs from most kung fu films because in the latter characters start from nothing and seem to carve out a destiny as they go along, whereas in his film, the destiny of the characters is clear from the beginning (Reynaud, "Entretien" 39). Once again, we see the heavy weight of time, the already lived, the forever past and thus forever fixed.

The film's plot, it must be admitted, is almost impossible to comprehend the first time through. What follows is the tentative description that I have been able to reconstruct after many viewings. Ouyang Feng, owing to some unknown event in his past, has exiled himself to the desert, where he makes a living as an assassin. Each year he is visited from the east by Huang Yaoshi, who, on this particular visit, offers him a special wine that will induce forgetfulness, but Ouyang refuses to indulge. He next meets Murong Yang (Brigitte Lin), who wants Ouyang to kill his friend Huang Yaoshi because he has jilted his sister, Murong Yin. Then Yin visits as well, asking Ouyang to murder her brother Yang because he has banished Huang, since he wants Yin all for himself. After several alternating visits, Ouyang finally concludes that Yin and Yang are the same, obviously disturbed (female) person.

The next part of the story begins with a visit by a poor but beautiful young woman (Charlie Young). She wants Ouyang to avenge her brother, who has been killed by soldiers, but all she has to offer in payment is a donkey and some eggs. Ouyang offers to do what she asks if she will give herself to him sexually, but she refuses, deciding instead to wait in front of his abode for someone more noble to appear. Ouyang tells us in voiceover that she reminds him of a woman from his past, the first hint of what has been troubling him. He is next visited by a mysterious figure played by Tony Leung Chiu-wai (who was Smirk in *Days of Being Wild* and who is not to be confused with Tony Leung Kar-fai, who plays Huang), an expert swordsman who is rapidly going blind. As in *The Seven Samurai*, the two men fight off bandits on behalf of some oppressed villagers who can only pay them a pittance, in several rousing action scenes. The blind swordsman then (apparently) returns to his wife (Carina Lau), who has been the focus of several flashbacks and voiceovers, and who seems to have earlier rejected him. It is only at this point that Ouyang realizes that the peach blossoms that the blind swordsman wanted to see one more time in his native village were really a reference to his wife, for this is her name.

Finally, a down-and-out warrior named Hong Qi (Jacky Cheung) teams up with Ouyang to defeat the bandits and even altruistically takes up the cause of the poor girl played by Charlie Young. He almost dies in the process, but eventually he returns to health and, now accompanied by his wife, departs. Ouyang realizes that compared to Hong Qi, life has made him cold and heartless. By the end of the film, his previous hurt is finally revealed: Not content to wait any longer for Ouyang while he prowled the land making his reputation, years earlier a beautiful woman (Maggie Cheung) married Ouyang's older brother instead. Only after she married did Ouyang realize that she was the love of his life and that he has missed out, forever condemning himself to emotional exile and an empty existence. Complicated connections between her and Huang, who is also in love with her and who has served, unknown to Ouyang, as a kind of emotional intermediary between them, are also revealed at this point. Finally, Ouyang learns that the woman has died two years earlier. He burns down his makeshift home in the desert, and the film ends.

The Kurosawa references, especially to *Seven Samurai*, are often explicit, and several of Wong's shot choices (for example, the overmatched professional fighters seen against the tattered banner that symbolizes their reduced prospects) seem to have been included expressly as acts of homage to the Japanese master. *Ashes* also feels like what have somewhat stupidly been called "spaghetti westerns," certainly in its visual terms and especially in its forlorn desert setting, its quasi-religious music track (replete with choirlike voices), and its narrative rhythm. And if the resolute, taciturn hero Ouyang Feng is a product of both *wuxia* and Sergio Leone, he also shares more than a few characteristics with the romantic, doomed gangster Ah Wah in *As Tears Go By*.

What Wong achieves in these characters, especially the world-weary Ouyang, whose life has been destroyed by thwarted love, is a fascinating blend of generic convention and his own particular (and ambivalent) romantic worldview. It's as though he is redirecting generic energies inherent in the form toward the elaboration of his own preoccupations. Hence, in an early title we read: "It's written in the Buddhist Canon: The flags are still, no wind blows, it's the heart of man that's in tumult!"

Genre thus becomes a vehicle for a more aesthetic expression of poetic ideas about life, love, memory, and loss.

A good example of the way that generic elements and an art-film concern for psychological realism can overlap comes in a remark that Wong made to Tony Rayns:

> Usually I find that genre conventions get in the way of dealing with certain areas of character psychology, but one of my inspirations for *Ashes of Time* was *The Searchers*—a film which suggests how you can get inside an apparently opaque protagonist. In Ford's film, I've always been extremely touched by the relationship between the John Wayne character and his sister-in-law, which you see only in the way she passes him a cloth.[10] It must amount to about three seconds of screen time, but the hint is enough. ("Poet" 14)

No stranger to the form, Wong seems to consider "kung fu films" a kind of overarching genre category with a number of subsets. And despite his occasional denigration of genre, it's clear in his remarks to Bérénice Reynaud, which deserve to be quoted at length, that he knew exactly what he was after:

> I didn't know whether I'd ever have the chance—or the desire—to make this kind of film again, so I put everything I knew and thought of this film genre in it. Now, my first experience of kung-fu epics came on the radio, and that's why there are so many monologues in the film. . . . During my childhood, these radio shows were one of the sources of my greatest pleasure. And then we stuffed ourselves on chivalric novels. And of course a huge number of these novels and radio shows were made into films. So I wanted to synthesize these different forms of the genre into my own version. (Reynaud, "Entretien" 39)

This blend of the generic and the personal subsequently manifests itself formally as well: "I also wanted to create a synthesis of different writing and directing styles. . . . In terms of the combat scenes, I filmed some in the style of Japanese martial arts, others were inspired by Chang Cheh, who was famous for his 'one-just-man-fighting-a-hundred' combat scenes, and others with elements of a more fantastic kung fu, where the combatants fly through the air" (Reynaud, "Entretien" 39).

Speaking with Michel Ciment, Wong goes even further, explaining how he varied the styles of fighting and the filming style according to each character and, in so doing, achieved art-film ends:

> Traditional martial arts films are designed to stimulate the senses of the spectator. I wanted to make mine a means of expressing the emotions of the characters. For example, when Brigitte Lin is swordfighting, it's like a dance. When I film Tony Leung Chiu-wai, the blind warrior, in slow motion, it's meant to suggest his weariness toward life, symbolized by the weight of his sword. Jacky Cheung, on the other hand, is filmed at 10 frames a second to suggest that he is emerging, that he is rising, in contrast to Tony Leung Chiu-wai, who is moving toward death. Some sequences were shot directly, while others, like those of Jacky Cheung, were done in the lab. (Ciment, "Entretien" 43)

This ostensibly antigeneric director of "art" films has clearly done his generic homework and demonstrates how attuned he is to his position in the history of the genre:

> Tsui Hark had brought the martial arts tradition back to the screen, a tradition so well illustrated earlier by King Hu with extraordinary ballets in the air, with the actors suspended on wires. But he was so often imitated that the style became sterile and ended up in an impasse. When I decided to shoot *Ashes of Time* I was determined not to go in this direction, since it seemed dead. With the exception of Brigitte Lin, whose actions are exaggerated, I wanted the other actors to fight on the ground so that their duels had a realistic feel, not an artificial one. (Ciment, "Entretien" 43)

But the film's visual strategy, naturally, exceeds the expression of generic concerns, and soon enough an overt tension is established between generic elements and whatever we might call their opposite. In fact, the film, which will quickly become obsessed with interiority, actually begins with a (purposely?) misleading barrage of visual and dramatic hyperstimulation, as, for example, the series of jump cuts that focus on the two opposing heroic figures, with heroic music on the sound track and cliffs blowing up all around them. The effect is to deliberately foreground Wong's directorial presence in a manner remarkably like more conventional Hong Kong cinema, thus adding to the self-consciousness that permeates the entire project and Hong King cinema more generally. What immediately follows is a series of scenes of sword fighting and martial arts, but this soon gives way to the psychological interiority that represents the bulk of the film.

As mentioned earlier, the plot is difficult to follow on a first viewing. For one thing, by complexly layering time and using what are apparently flashbacks within flashbacks, Wong seems to be attempting to re-create, within the viewer, the achronological state of mind of the characters. The jump cuts of the opening sequences also signal the dislocations of plot and characterization that are to follow, and the striking montage sequence is impressive but difficult to construct a narrative around. (Later, minor sequences, such as chopsticks falling from a table, are shown with the cuts purposely out of order.) This opening montage has been termed "Eisensteinian" by more than one critic, and it is, at least for the first several shots, which dialectically oppose East and West, the two terms embodied in the characters and in the title. But the sequence quickly abandons the strict oppositional logic of the Russian director in favor of a surrealistic juxtaposition of seemingly random, largely expressive fragments. In this, Wong's film recalls more than anything else Buñuel's cinematic experimentation in films like *Un Chien Andalou*, especially in the time indicators ("three months later," "last spring") that, since they are never firmly anchored deictically, seem narratively meaningless.

Even the extreme long shots leading up to battle scenes, which are meant to convey a visual meaning something like "an impossible number of warriors riding toward the hero," are, owing to the extreme foreshortening effect of the long lens, cramped into tight frames that close off and constrict space rather than open it up. Shots like these have the contradictory effect of making the film appear to be more a visualization of the interior, psychological experience of the narrator, principally Ouyang Feng, rather than part of an independent, epic narration. The slow-motion or stretch-printed martial arts sequences (actually few in number) work in this same constricted direction yet simultaneously convey a great deal of latent, pent-up energy as well.

These restrained, in some ways purposely frustrating shots of powerful movement that never seems to move are magnificently answered by static, extreme long shots in which nothing is seen by the immobile camera but a single man and a single tree, say, artfully and self-consciously arranged against a gorgeous horizon and a grand and expressive sky. A similar sort of contrast is accomplished by punctuating the constant visual stimulation and dynamic movement in some shots (curtains blowing, a spinning birdcage) with absolutely still images in other shots in which all seems frozen dead. (An alternate rhythm consists of dynamic camera movement within a shot in which the figures and objects are stationary.)

Ackbar Abbas has also noticed this visual expressivity: "It is no longer a choreography of action that we see, as in other kung fu or gangster movies, but a composition of light and color, into which all action has dissolved; a kind of Abstract Expressionism or Action Painting. Action has now become non-figurative" (60). Stephen Teo has likewise spoken of the film's "impressionist quality" and mentioned the "pastel lighting" that "recalls motifs from Chinese painting, pointed up appropriately by the desert location and other more temperate landscapes (creeks, ponds). The slow-motion action scenes convey a feeling of an artist daubing paint freely on a canvas" (199).

These shots and others like them thus clearly impact the graphic question that we have been exploring. When viewers are pushed up this close, as it were, against a flat visual field, what they experience, chiefly, is dynamic contours and forms, line and shapes, rather than discrete narrative events. This effect is even more strongly felt since the expressive, rarely naturalistic primary colors (red and blue especially) are back from Wong's first film, *As Tears Go By*, after having been muted in *Days of Being Wild*.

One place this can particularly be seen is in the faces of many of Wong's female stars—Carina Lau and Maggie Cheung in this film— which become iconic and strangely de-realized through these patches of vibrant primary colors that make up the white of their faces, the black of their hair, and the red of their lips. This particular denaturalization effect is enhanced by an intensity of line and form, abetted by high key lighting; but elsewhere, the same expressive result is achieved, within the tight interiors, when objects or people pass so close to the camera that they are out of focus, hence unrecognizable, mere white blurs that seem reduced to their affective content and even more strangely resonant for their indistinctness. The result of all this is that the viewer can momentarily forget the specific twists of narrative and causality and become simply immersed in the flow of the blurred images in any given sequence. One knows that murder and mayhem are occurring, but one is never *visually* certain as to who has the advantage and who is doing exactly what to whom, as in several of the fight scenes in this film and in *As Tears Go By.* (Of course, the generic, narrative assumption leads us unconsciously to believe that the hero is winning, even if we can't exactly *see* it.)

A formal complexity also arises here that first appeared in *As Tears Go By*, where it was utilized more for raw sensation and thus remained much less tied to thematic concerns. I'm referring to the complicated, contrapuntal rhythm occasioned by the mesh of the sound effects (clanging swords, overturned furniture, grunts, shots), which can't, by definition, be artificially stretched and still be comprehensible, and the visuals, which can be purposely blurred at an infinite variety of speeds and yet remain at least somewhat intelligible. In other words, an exact overlap of slow-motion or stretch-printed visuals with matching blurred sounds simply wouldn't work, and Wong doesn't even try.

What results from this gap or apparent contradiction between the two tracks is a strange interior tension that has a powerful, if unconscious, effect on the viewer. This tension is a result of the fact that while the sound is mostly naturalistic, it is accompanied by visuals that clearly are not. (A similar effect is created in Richard Linklater's animated film *Waking Life* [2001], in which animated sequences clash provocatively and productively with the completely realistic sound and dialogue track.)

This tension also effectively breaks up the "natural" linkage between visual and sound tracks that conventionally serves to create a sense of wholeness and convincing presence in the image.[11] Despite Wong's claim that in most of his fighting sequences he was aiming for realism and sought to avoid artifice, the entire project of *Ashes of Time* is marked by a clear and purposeful artificiality that continually calls attention to the manufactured nature of what we are watching.[12]

Finally, and most importantly, the gap between the two tracks also deconstructs time itself, creating a gap within it, since the sound is still in "real" time, and must be, if it is to be intelligible and to signify cognitively and narratively, whereas the visuals construct their own complex, expressive time that is more elastic than clock time. The subjectivity of time and our relation to the past are precisely what the film is about, as it creatively manipulates these entities in its very structure. Abetting this effect is the juxtaposition of multiple time periods, a technique by which the viewer comes to experience the same irregular but generative chronological relations as the characters.

On the aural level beyond the sound effects, this is the first film by Wong to use through-composed music, as befits such a big-budget production, rather than the pop songs taken from a variety of decades and styles that had marked his first two films (Ungerböck 28). Wong also transcends the powerful but reticent voiceovers of *Days of Being Wild* to attain a new level of density and affect. Some critics consider the voiceover inherently anticinematic (or a telltale sign of a weakly constructed narrative), but in its attempt to defeat the cinema's age-old difficulty with conveying interior states, it can serve to expand the repertory of cinematic techniques.[13] Yet it's also true—and to my mind this is its great strength—that the voiceover technique can bring in something from "outside" cinema, the powerful suggestiveness and allusiveness that only artfully arranged words, that is to say, poetry, can provide. In this film, the effect is accomplished through the use of the evocative motif of the "peach blossom" that circulates throughout as flowering tree, proper name, memory, and location, trailing a stream of rich connotations and reminding us of the similarly allusive, though more ambivalent, bird motif in *Days of Being Wild*. This appropriately self-conscious motif serves also to juxtapose the characters and to make them (always purposely, of course) blur and blend. The verbal poetry is further enhanced through its association with the "poetic" visuals that reign supreme in this film, demonstrating once again the intimate expressive connections that can obtain between the linguistic and the visual.

These powerful and complicated visual and aural techniques have been marshalled by Wong in support of his by now well-established thematic concerns. From the very first, the director's signature themes of the impossibility of love and the even greater impossibility of recapturing the past, or, more precisely, of undoing the mistakes of the past, reappear. Huang touts his magical memory-erasing wine to Ouyang because "man's biggest problem is that he remembers the past." How much better it would be to forget everything that has gone before, he says, because each day would be a new beginning. After Huang drinks the magic wine, all seems forgotten, and while he is asleep, an unknown

[margin handwritten note: these critics' idea is "interior," i.e. cinema includes sound as a primary element]

woman's hand extends into the frame. This is followed by a fleeting glance, apparently an image disappearing from Huang's memory, of a woman moving softly away down a dark corridor. Only little by little, as we reconstruct the past ourselves, will we learn Ouyang's sad story, and that of the others, and what painful memories they are all trying to erase. Near the end, when the film focuses on Ouyang's real love (the nameless character played by Maggie Cheung), we hear her bitter lament about having married Ouyang's brother, which serves as the emotional high point of this particular theme:

> Nothing matters, because everything changes. I thought I had won, then one day I saw the face of a loser in the mirror. I failed to be with the one I loved in the best years of my life. If we could only go back to the past. . . .

By the end of the film, Ouyang is back exactly as we first saw him, pitching his services as an assassin to an unknown potential client. Here Wong uses the same shot as in the beginning, suggesting the eternal immutability of life and its endless circularity. However, by the end, Ouyang, like Proust's narrator, has learned that there is one saving grace after all. Far from being the source of all trouble, he tells us, our sole advantage is *memory,* for it is the best and only way to hold on to the precious things that one has lost in life.

Love, like the past, is another site of impossibility. In this sad tale, no one is satisfied, and everyone is frustrated. When Michel Ciment suggested to Wong that betrayal is the theme of the film, the director corrected him to say that the theme is rejection. Ouyang, as he admits in his voiceover, rejects others first so as not to be rejected himself; Murong Yin creates a brother because she has been rejected by Huang; the blind swordsman has been rejected by his wife, whom he still loves, and thus self-destruction is the only possibility for him. Huang loves the woman who pines for Ouyang but never speaks of his love for fear of being rejected. According to the director, the only two characters who escape this self-destructive logic are Hong Qi and the girl with the eggs who seeks revenge for her brother's murder: "Both of them will have a happy destiny by the end and they will influence [Ouyang] in his decision to leave the desert in the final images of the film. I'm realizing

Figure 4. *Ashes of Time*: Hong Qi (Jacky Cheung),
the ethical warrior, stares ahead at his fate.

while saying all this that it's a thread that runs throughout all my films, this idea of rejection" (Ciment, "Entretien" 44).

It might be objected that the whole enterprise of *Ashes of Time* is saturated with a heavy privileging of romantic love that, given the time period of arranged marriages in which it is set, is anachronistic. As we saw earlier, however, Wong is not particularly interested in historical authenticity for its own sake, clearly preferring to use the past and generic conventions as symbolic tools for expressing his sense of the present.

Other familiar romantic motifs make their first appearance here as well. One example is the desire, traditionally coded as male, to explore the world beyond the boundaries of one's own locality, to test oneself. We see this in Ouyang's internal debate, uttered in voiceover, between Hong Qi's youthful, perhaps naive, enthusiasm to discover what's on "the other side of the mountain" and Ouyang's own world-weary pessimism. At first, Ouyang indicates that Hong's impulse will always be futile, and the film seems to agree with him, since what has been abandoned always turns out to be exactly what was being sought in the first place. Yet Ouyang also comes to understand that it is this irrepressible desire itself, perhaps because it is naive, that gives meaning to life and that must be indulged if one is to be anything but an empty shell. "Once I could have been like Hong, but I failed," he tells us bitterly.

The characters overlap and repeat each other, and we come to realize that the film is not only about memory and the past but also, as in *Days of Being Wild*, about identity, which is always a function of memory and the past, as the British philosopher John Locke pointed out long ago. The question is also raised, especially in the powerful but supremely delicate sex scene between Yin and Ouyang, that given the complexity of psyche and memory, who are we really making love to when we make love? (The mentally disturbed Yin thinks or is pretending that her lover is Huang, but Ouyang too comments, "Her hands were soft, like my brother's wife.") When the blind swordsman encounters the girl with the eggs crying, he wonders aloud whether his wife, whom she reminds him of, would cry for him. Hong Qi abandons Ouyang, saying that he lost his "real self" by associating with Ouyang, a man who would never risk his life for some eggs. When Ouyang realizes that Yin and Yang are the same person, he comments that "in this dual identity was a wounded soul." Wong is raising some postmodern questions concerning the nature of subjectivity and the status of the individual self. As Stokes and Hoover put it in describing, with a Marxist twist, the subjective dynamics of the film, "the permutations of character traits and resonances between characters describe fluid identities and selfhoods created by contingency, not distinctive individuals but a collective persona reflective of human beings coexisting over time" (188).

Sticking, however, with the specifics of the film, there comes a lovely moment in another scene that sums up this liquidity of self, replete with haunting music on the sound track, when Yin murmurs, "Yes, I know you, you promised to marry me." Appropriately, we can't see who's in the dark in the background, and while we may hope that it is Huang, we know, deep down, that it is only Ouyang substituting for him. "Even if it's not true, say that you love me the most," she continues. Then the figure in the background reveals that he is indeed Ouyang. "What woman do you love the most?" she asks. "You, of course," is his gallant and altogether appropriate reply.

As with Wong's earlier films, some critics have developed a detailed contemporary political reading of *Ashes of Time*, but these efforts have not been entirely convincing and sometimes smack of special pleading. Stokes and Hoover, for example, are impressed by the contrast between the sword-fighting scenes and "the scenery itself [that] represents a void, a landscape of absence contextualized only by the human activity in it. As such the film metaphorically portrays contemporary Hong Kong as both dream fantasy and nightmare" (189). In their reading, Ouyang's way station becomes a stand-in for the colony itself, a nonplace between the departing British and the soon-to-arrive Chinese. While one doesn't want to give aid and comfort to those who believe that all political interpretations of putative "artistic" films are inherently mistaken, it must nevertheless be pointed out that Wong has said, in response to a question concerning his choice of location, that "my principle goal was to find a desert which could function as a symbol for the emotional state of the characters" (Reynaud, "Entretien" 39).

Much of the effort to develop a political interpretation of the film, not surprisingly, revolves around the character of Ouyang Feng, who becomes somewhat unrecognizable in the process. Stokes and Hoover, for example, claim that

Figure 5. *Ashes of Time*: Ouyang Feng (Leslie Cheung) indulges in some fancy swordwork.

the characterization of Ouyang Feng, tied to a past not of his own making, and waiting to make a future, personifies Hong Kong. Eventually he will choose to burn the way station and leave the desert behind, but first he must work through his current circumstances. Having turned his back on swordfighting, he is a deal-making middleman who bridges the gap between sole proprietor and transnational capitalist. (190)

Summarizing, they say that "Ouyang must, paradoxically, learn to remember and forget; that is, to recognize the past which has formed him but to bend it in the present to face his future—like Hong Kong" (191). Tsui sees the film (and Ouyang, whom he calls a "postmodern capitalist") as virtually *only* about Hong Kong and the takeover (104–12). He also offers an overly rigid interpretation of the eggs proffered by the character played by Charlie Young, for example, as "symbolic of birth and new life" (110), apparently forgetting that Hong Qi eats them all, and, in any case, eggs that are reserved for eating are those that are devoid of new life.

David Bordwell's response to these political readings provides a welcome corrective, even if he perhaps exaggerates in the other direction: "To treat these lovelorn films as abstract allegories of Hong Kong's historical situation risks losing sight of Wong Kar-wai's naked appeal to our feelings about young romance, its characteristic dilemmas, moods, and moves" (*Planet* 280). Wong's films are about much more than "young romance," but special pleading and tortuous political interpretations aren't especially useful in helping us describe them. It seems absolutely clear, however, that a political reading of Wong's subsequent films, beginning with the next one under consideration, *Chungking Express*, is not only plausible but crucial. Even there, however, as we shall see, Wong's films can't and shouldn't be constrained within a purely political rubric.

Chungking Express

Chungking Express, initially regarded as little more than a peppy bagatelle slapped together during a two-month break near the end of the arduous making of *Ashes of Time*, ironically became the film that first brought Wong Kar-wai international attention. Many conflicting reasons for the crippling hiatus of *Ashes of Time* have been adduced by various commentators, including Wong himself, but the most plausible came in the director's interview with Michel Ciment in 1995: "We had a two month delay while we waited for some equipment to redo the sound: it had been recorded in the desert and it was very bad. Since I had nothing else to do, I decided to make *Chungking Express* just following my instincts" ("Entretien" 44).

Where *Ashes* is serious and gratifyingly deliberate, *Chungking Express*, which Chuck Stephens has called "bubblegum cinema," is a lighthearted, contemporary romp through the same themes of time, love, and loss that had obsessed Wong in the earlier film. Just as in the martial arts epic, virtually all the characters in *Chungking Express* pine for someone they've lost or can't have, and the men suffer, if possible, even more violently than the women.

In the first part of the film, Takeshi Kaneshiro plays lovelorn undercover policeman number 223[14] (he also tells us, almost as an afterthought, that his name is He Qiwu), who has been dumped by his girlfriend May. Cop 223 spends much of his half of the film buying cans of pineapple whose sell-by date of May 1 corresponds with his birthday and the one-month anniversary of his breakup with May. Impetuously, he vows (in voiceover) to fall in love with the next woman who walks into the bar in which he is drowning his sorrows. Conveniently, it's the unnamed woman (Brigitte Lin) that we've been following as she goes about her drug-smuggling business in a blonde wig. (Her scheme to have Indians smuggle drugs for her is betrayed by the participants, and her Anglo drug-dealer boss has threatened to kill her if she doesn't recover the drugs.) This potential amorous encounter between Cop 223 and the Lin character also ends unhappily, however, as the worn-out Lin (she's had to settle many scores along the way) falls asleep in their hotel room, and 223 finds himself more alone than ever. The hotel food he tries to console himself with doesn't help. Nevertheless, the birthday greetings she pages to him the next day offer a ray of hope.

The second half of the film concerns a uniformed policeman (number 633), played by Tony Leung Chiu-wai, who was the blind swordsman in *Ashes of Time*. He too has been rejected by his girlfriend, a flight attendant (Valerie Chow), and, like 223, he seeks solace in the fast-food joint called Midnight Express, where he meets Faye (the neophyte actress and rock star Faye Wong), a particularly fey young woman who works there. She quickly becomes obsessed with 633's private life and apartment, to which she has access once the departing flight attendant drops off his keys at the Midnight Express. Faye ends up completely redoing his apartment, though he seems to attribute all the changes he encounters to the power of the inanimate objects found therein. When he finally notices her and asks her out on a date—they're to meet at the California Bar—she leaves him a message that she's decided to go off to the real California instead. However, she promises to return in a year. When she does, it's as a flight attendant herself. She goes to the Midnight Express to discover that 633 is the new owner, preparing for a grand reopening. At the very end, it seems that maybe they will get together after all.

The title nicely encapsulates both halves of the film: According to Tsui, "Chungking" represents the first story, which is set in the "Chungking flophouses" of Kowloon, and "Express" refers to the fast-food place, Midnight Express, which is located in central Hong Kong's version of SoHo, Lan Kwai Fong (115). Ackbar colorfully describes the Chungking Mansions, where most of the first half of the film takes place, as "a dingy, down-market, mall-cum-flophouse, incredibly located right in the midst of Tsimshatsui, Hong Kong's most expensive tourist area. It is a truly heterotopic space and living contradiction" (66).

All the characters of *Chungking Express* are lonely and isolated, as in Wong's previous films, and at least one of them, Faye, hopes for salvation elsewhere, in California of all places (a running comic motif has her playing "California Dreamin'" throughout the film at ear-splitting levels because "it stops me from thinking"). In a confessional moment, she tells 633, "I just want to enjoy life," and she seems to entertain no higher aspirations. Cop 633 entertainingly devotes himself to makeshift attempts to create companions out of the objects that surround him in his living space—a bar of soap that "needs more confidence," a "sobbing" washcloth he describes as lacking in "strength and absorbency," a shirt, an apartment that "cries," some stuffed animals—and these futile attempts are simultaneously sad and funny. Cop 223's story does achieve a modest happy ending of sorts—or at least one that is the most that can be expected in this fallen world—when he retrieves the birthday greeting that the Brigitte Lin character has left for him with his message service. "Now I'll remember her all my life," he tells us fervently. Clearly, we aren't all that far from the forlorn inhabitants of *Ashes of Time*, but things have, in fact, changed, as Wong told Bérénice Reynaud. Whereas in his earlier films, characters are dissatisfied by their loneliness, he said, "*Chungking Express* represents a real break: the characters accept their loneliness, they're more independent, and they see in their quest not a kind of despair but a kind of amusement" (Reynaud, "Entretien" 38).

One of the most innovative aspects of *Chungking Express* is to be found in its dual narratives. Besides neatly dividing the film in two, the two stories also feature similar plots and similar characters—like his earlier films, but more outrageously—and contain many overlapping features. The fast-food place known as Midnight Express provides a kind of still center—itself significantly centered on that favorite Wongian topos, food—a spatial *point de repère* for all the characters. The two stories constantly refer to each other, and we are more or less "handed off" from the first story to the second when 223, almost touching Faye while passing her in front of the Midnight Express, comments in his voiceover (with the image in freeze-frame), "I passed .01cm from her, and six hours later she fell in love with another man," meaning 633, who is meanwhile lounging at the left of the frame. Cop 223 had said the same thing—only reversed—when he almost knocked down Brigitte Lin while chasing a criminal in the beginning of the film: "I passed just .01cm from her, but 57 hours later, I fell in love with this woman." (How he knows this, while passing her this first time, remains a mystery. It is as though the voiceover commentary is occurring later, while 223 is himself watching the film we're watching.)

The overlapping of narratives is also reflected in the doubling of various characters, another favorite Wong technique. Two of the many similar-looking women in the film, for example, are confusingly named May. Furthermore, the bar girl whom we see with the Anglo bartender/drug dealer seems like a downscale double of the Brigitte Lin character, since both sport flamboyant blonde wigs. In the context of her sleazy Anglo boyfriend, who is Lin's boss, the wig suggests that the bar girl is trying to conform to the bartender's racial expectations. Significantly, when Lin kills him at the end of the first half of the film, Lin drops her wig in the foreground of the frame, the climactic final gesture of this section of the

Figure 6. *Chungking Express*: Faye (Faye Wong) doubled, like so much else in this film, this time in the metal surface of an escalator.

film, as though she had merged with her alter ego and was declaring their joint independence from the drug dealer's depredations.

And if you look very, very closely, you can see that even in the first part of the film, 633 appears for a few seconds (before we know who he is, of course) hanging over the railing of a subway station. Also Faye, the fast-food counter girl from part two, at one point in part one walks out of a store, past Lin, with a big stuffed Garfield cat in her arms. (Wong told Ciment that "for me, [Lin] is the same woman [as Faye] ten years later" ["Entretien" 45].) Much of this playful doubling is related to the ubiquity of chance, the theme that has animated so many recent commercial films (*Sliding Doors; Run, Lola, Run; Me, Myself, and I,* and so on) and that is derived from its ultimate source, films by the late Polish master Kzrystof Kieslowski like *The Double Life of Veronique* and the *Three Colors* trilogy. (Curtis K. Tsui also claims to have spotted a shot of the flight attendant in part one, but I haven't been able to find this shot myself. In any case, his conclusion that these appearances might mean that the two stories are actually *simultaneous* rather than consecutive is convincing, especially in light of a small discovery of my own, achieved by dint of the still function on my DVD player: In part two, Faye, for just a second of unemphasized screen time, places beside 633's bed the Garfield cat that we saw her buying in part one; 633 is also later seen talking to this stuffed animal.)

In addition, both Lin and Faye have a penchant for falling asleep at crucial moments in their narratives, and by the end of the film Faye ends up becoming a flight attendant, just like 633's previous girlfriend. Earlier, 633 explains to us in voiceover how he used to taunt this girlfriend while she hid in the closet, causing her to pop out suddenly; at this very moment in his monologue, Faye, who is hiding there now, pops out the same way, though he doesn't see her. While massaging Faye's legs in a later scene, he talks about having performed the same service for his earlier girlfriend. It is possible to see this frequent doubling of women as a misogynistic flattening, suggesting that all women are ultimately interchangeable, but since it's true of the men in *Chungking Express* as well, something else seems to be going on, something about the fluidity of individual identity. It's almost as though subjectivity becomes utterly porous in a contemporary "heterotopic" urban environment like Hong Kong, as when Faye asks innocently in her voiceover, "Can dreams be catching?"

The connections continue. Though the humorous/serious expiration-date motif is primarily attached to 223, the Anglo drug dealer uses an almost-expired can as a signal to Lin that her time is running short, and when she kills him at the end of part one, the camera settles on the same tin of Portuguese sardines lying next to his body, which has the same expiration date, May 1, that 223 has been fixated on. At one point, 223 rhetorically asks a tired convenience-store employee about what the expired cans must feel like when they are thrown away, a humorous anthropomorphization that looks forward to 633's conversations with sundry inanimate objects in his apartment. Cop 223 looks at some goldfish in one scene, a gesture that points to the goldfish that Faye will bring to 633's apartment later on. Near the end of the film, 633 has to resurrect the letter he has thrown away in order to reconnect with Faye, just as 223 at first abandons the pager that will end up bringing some solace to his love life, and 633 goes to a convenience store, 223's favorite hangout, to piece it back together. As David Bordwell has pointed out, the parallelism of the two male epiphanies at end of the two parts of the film is enhanced by the fact that both take place in the rain, and both scenes are pictorially composed in a parallel fashion (*Planet* 288).

Besides the intricacy of the narrative connections and the doubling mesh of characters, Wong, reverting to his ambivalent fascination for the cool attractiveness of Yuddy in *Days of Being Wild*, is also obviously taken with the surface beauty of his actors. It's true that the director perversely disguises and even brutalizes Brigitte Lin in a fashion reminiscent of the treatment of Maggie Cheung in *As Tears Go By*—there the disfiguring face mask, now a grotesque blonde wig and both a raincoat and sunglasses (her character's laconic explanation for the contradiction: "Who knows when it will rain or when it will turn out sunny?"). But it's also true that Takeshi Kaneshiro, the half-Japanese pop star who plays 223 (note the self-reflexive joke when 223 tells us that his ex-girlfriend May wanted him to be more like a Japanese pop star, which is precisely what he is in real life), and the Taiwanese pop star Faye Wong are both almost overwhelmingly cute and meant to seduce us immediately. In fact, it's clear that Wong's camera is especially fascinated by Faye Wong. (Quentin Tarantino, in an introduction to the VHS version of the film, confesses to a similar obsession.) But for this viewer, at least, Faye's insouciant cuteness (a clear homage to the gamine Jean Seberg in Godard's *Breathless*) is laid on a bit thick when she gambols fetchingly through 633's apartment for what can seem like hours. Yet even a fault like this, apparently, can be recuperated, as when Eugene Chew interestingly if not entirely convincingly claims that "the cuteness and mugging of [Wong's] stars is not cheap affectation but the accurate representation of the freeplay and barter of identities so essential to the Hong Kong character."

Chew's reference brings us to the political aspect of the film, which is, for once, undeniable. Since *Chungking Express* is actually set in present-day Hong Kong, there is a clear political subtext to whatever happens in it. Tsui plausibly claims that the film's mostly humorous expiration-date motif, for example, refers to the expiration of Hong Kong as a British colony (116), though his specific political microreadings of the various relationships and characters seem, as usual, rather strained and unconvincing. In interviews, Wong has vaguely linked the political issue with a more general urban alienation that has come to seem normal: "*Days of Being Wild* centers on various feelings about staying in or leaving Hong Kong. That's less of an issue now that we're so close to 1997. *Chungking Express* is more about the way people feel now. In *Days*, the characters are not happy with their solitude; it's the same with the characters in *Ashes of Time*. The people in *Chungking* know how to entertain themselves, even if it's just by talking to a bar of soap. They know how to live in a city" (Rayns, "Poet" 14).

Gina Marchetti sees the film's obsessive time references (including the frequently repeated song "What a Difference a Day Makes")—as well as the fact that everyone seems to have a boarding pass and is considering whether to stay or leave—as clearly related to the 1997 handover (290–91). "Under the veneer of popular optimism about the future," she points out, "there is also a sense that Hong Kong has been abandoned and, worse, that, like the jilted lover, it has no power or say in this decision" (291).

Stokes and Hoover typically offer a more detailed political reading, focusing on the privatization of consumption by utilizing Marx's analysis of the way in which commodities disguise the social relations of the human beings who made them. Consequently, they make much of the fact that Faye imports new commodities into 633's apartment and that 633 enjoys talking to his commodities (198–99). They claim that the unconventional coming together of the two couples in the film is also significant because it "defines a new way of uniting that has meaning for the particular time and place—Hong Kong on the verge of its return to the Mainland, as well as the couples who make a conscious decision to be together in these uncertain postmodern times" (200). This last formulation, if somewhat syntactically blurry, strikes the right analytic balance between Wong's concerns about the specific political moment in Hong Kong and his more generalized view of contemporary urban life.

Whatever political interest the film might hold, however, it is clear that, once again, its amazing energy derives chiefly from Wong's brilliantly innovative use of visual images and sound. The film throws the viewer immediately and quite viscerally into what has become Wong's aesthetic signature, the stretch printing of action scenes accompanied by heavily inflected music on the soundtrack and even more strongly accented sound effects. The powerful kinetic effect of the opening chase scene involving 223, for example, is stunning and stays with us throughout the film, especially as the technique is reproduced several more times. Most of the film was shot with a handheld camera, a decision that accords perfectly with its location in a crowded, tense urban environment. At times the filming feels almost like a throwback to the self-conscious "veracity" of Italian neorealism, as what are obviously real walls and doorways crowd into the frame, often obscuring the camera's vision.

Paradoxically, however, this apparently heightened realism functions in the context of utterly purposeful stylization and thus serves more as an expressive device than some sort of privileged access to the real. More blatantly expressive techniques are used elsewhere to indicate interior psychological states, as when a blurry, repeated reflection of Faye in a metal wall on screen right eventually takes over nearly the whole of the image. One hesitates to assign a precise narrative or symbolic meaning here—this usually amounts to diminishing an image's interest and power—but it is clear that something of Faye's inner turmoil and unsteady subjectivity is being suggested.

One other especially striking audiovisual technique—a technique new to Wong's films—occurs twice, both times in the second story. The first time, 633 and Faye are shown standing absolutely still, as though frozen, while a horde of anonymous Hong Kongers, all in a blur, soundlessly passes in front of them. The second time, a similarly faceless crowd blurs around a reflective and melancholy 633, standing all alone in a bar, his image remaining distinct. One effect of this new technique is to add to the visual, graphic expressivity, related to that of abstract painting, that we have been tracing throughout this study. It also seems to signify or illustrate, in a novel visual way, the old theme of lonely individual isolation in the midst of the pulsating anonymous crowd, without having to resort to more conventional narrative means. Speaking specifically (if somewhat cryptically) about this technique, Wong has said, "I read something that said 'in order to show change, you have to use things that are immortal.' Time goes by, people change, but many things don't change. Maybe I'm so interested in time because, as a filmmaker, I always have so many deadlines. But despite all that, there's one thing that doesn't ever change, and that's the desire people have to communicate with others" (Reynaud, "Entretien" 39).

The powerfully kinetic opening sequence is followed by the equally lively but more comic scene centering on the Indian workers who betray

Lin's drug-smuggling scheme. Especially noteworthy is the humorous use of Indian music; once again it's clear that music, and sound in general, is just as important to Wong's films as the visuals, and the two tracks used in innovative tandem gives such brio to his particular postmodern style. Tsui has nicely summarized Wong's bravura use of sound in the film, providing a useful sociopolitical spin at the same time:

> The score is an almost discordant mix of up-to-the-moment synthesizer cues, wailing electric guitars, source music from various ethnicities, Hindi chanting, and various pop songs. Even the languages spoken by the characters intermix freely (at one point, Cop 223 asks the smuggler if she "likes pineapple" in Cantonese, Japanese, English, and Mandarin). As with the film's visual imagery, the viewer is provided with a sonic tapestry evoking a polyglot culture that is very much the Crown Colony. (114–15)

A good—and amusing—example of this multilevel "composedness" occurs in 633's sexy scene with his flight attendant lover. While he plays with a model airplane, we simultaneously hear two entirely different things on the sound track, the western song "What a Difference a Day Makes" and a dispassionate, recorded British-accented voice rehearsing airline safety procedures. The latter, which is completely out of context, is accompanied by the scantily clad flight attendant's provocative demonstration of the procedures.

Though Wong often privileges audio/visual expressivity over narrative structure, in *Chungking Express* the figural dimension seems to take over almost completely. The French critic Jean-Marc Lalanne has an insightful view of this dynamic that accords well with the emphasis on graphic expressivity that underlies this book. "In cutting and recomposing through editing each movement of the actors, the mise-en-scène invents a kind of 'ballet mécanique' of human movements, a choreography in which each gesture becomes abstract, loses its functionality in favor of a purely musical value" (Lalanne, "Deux" 40).

As the necessary underpinning for these visual and aural effects, location is once again supremely important. A similar fascination with urban textures marked Wong's first and second films, but now these textures seem to have become all. In many ways, *Chungking Express* is a love letter to Wong's vitally frenetic hometown, Hong Kong, and

Figure 7. *Chungking Express*: Cop 633 (Tony Leung Chui-wai) and stewardess (Valerie Chow) playing games in bed.

its wonderfully garish lights and colors—which in this film are orange and chartreuse and other aggressive hues—as well as to the ubiquity of its sensual pleasures, especially those of the culinary variety, which are always about more than just eating. Wong told Ciment that he shot the film in the Chungking House quarter of Hong Kong because "this overpopulated and hyperactive place is a good metaphor for the city itself" (Ciment, "Entretien" 45).

Accompanying this emphasis on the specificity of Hong Kong is a new interest in American products and companies like Coca-Cola, Kent cigarettes, McDonald's, Del Monte, M&Ms, and United Airlines, references to which are ubiquitous. This gesture, however, seems not to be intended as a critique of American cultural imperialism à la Wim Wenders in *Im Lauf der Zeit* (Kings of the Road; 1976), in which one character complains to another that "the Americans have colonized our minds," but rather as an authentic portrayal of the nature of contemporary global popular culture. These are quasi-universal signifiers, in other words, that have apparently broken free from their original American signifieds, though the economic connection always remains in force at some level, hidden under the flashy, "innocent" surface. As Marchetti has pointed out, behind the stylish love story and all the American pop culture is "another story about economics and the politics of identity" (289).

The most important manifestation of this ubiquitous global culture comes in Faye's devotion to the song "California Dreamin'," which is played virtually incessantly throughout the second half of the film, while another American song of an earlier vintage, "What a Difference a Day Makes," comes to represent the relationship between 633 and the flight attendant. The inclusion of these songs does not seem to represent a cynical commercial calculation on Wong's part to make the film more international in appeal. Rather, it is simply a sign that young people in Hong Kong, and virtually everywhere else in the world today—for better or worse—communicate with themselves and with each other increasingly through this now deracinated globalized American culture.

Structuring cinematic motifs of a quasi-literary nature appear again in this film, but the space they occupy is more comic or ironic than in Wong's earlier work. Cop 633's affair with the flight attendant is playfully and consistently described in terms of the language of aviation—flights, takeoffs, landings, and so on ("change of flight—your plane cancelled" reads the note in which she informs him she's dumping him)—as is much else in the film. And instead of the bird that tragically cannot stop flying—or that has been dead all along—that we encountered in *Days of Being Wild,* Wong's central motif is now the repeated temporal marker of a sell-by date, a humorous signifier of chronology that nevertheless powerfully suggests time's utter implacability, both on a philosophical level and on the specific political level of the handover of the colony to the People's Republic.[15] Throughout, various voiceover narrators obsessively recount other typically Wongian narrative time markers ("In 56 hours I would fall in love with her"; "Six hours later she fell in love with him"; "Two minutes from now I will be 25," and so on), as recurring clock numbers click over, incessantly ticking off the minutes, hours, and days. Memory, once again, becomes the means by which we organize time and our very subjectivity itself. Near the end of the first part of the film, 223 asks rhetorically in voiceover, "Is there anything in the world that doesn't have an expiry date? If memories could be canned, would they also have expiry dates? If so, I hope they last for centuries." As Howard

Hampton succinctly puts it, in this film, "even as life is happening, it's experienced as memory" (91).

What is perhaps ultimately most interesting and most different about *Chungking Express* is that all of its manifold complexities unfold within the airiest of contexts. Even the sometimes irascible but always illuminating David Bordwell ends up liking this film and places it for us usefully within the Hong Kong cinematic tradition: "Wong revivifies the formula. Instead of tightening up the plot, he slackens it beyond even Hong Kong's episodic norm, letting a fine network of parallels and recurring motifs come forward. Deeply indebted to popular tradition, committed to a conception of light cinema, his confection nourishes all filmmakers who dream of movies that are at once experimental and irresistibly enjoyable" (*Planet* 289).

But it's even more than this, I think. Does this film, and *Fallen Angels,* the one that follows it, perhaps point toward a new, nonnarrative, antirealist, hyperstylized place that the cinema of the future will occupy? Perhaps. Here is the way that the visionary Jean-Marc Lalanne puts it:

> *Chungking Express,* like *Fallen Angels,* strives to haul cinema out of the cinema, to connect it to different sites, those carrying the large flows of new images, of audio-visual and of virtual reality. To spin out the Borgesian metaphor, the new territories mapped out by Wong Kar-wai are the abstract regions of modern communications; a land of images where cinema's mystique, as an art of registering, would cease to have any meaning, where images would seem to be self-engendered, deploying themselves without any reference to the real. ("Images" 14)

Fallen Angels

Wong's next film, *Fallen Angels* (1995), seems on first viewing to be little more than a replay of motifs and themes that predominated in his earlier films and, more specifically, a mere rehash of the frenetic style of *Chungking Express,* as many of his critics have been eager to point out. Yet this analysis has not always been as deep as it could be, and many commentators seem to assume that Wong is unaware of these repetitions, as though they were completely unintentional. While I think that the film does represent something of an artistic dead end for the director—his next effort, *Happy Together*, will take him in a very different direction—*Fallen Angels* is a much richer and more innovative work than it at first appears.

Part of what makes it feel repetitious is the fact that it is based partially on a story line originally intended for *Chungking Express* (the hit man and his female dispatcher), which didn't make it into the earlier film. Like the finished version of *Chungking Express*, furthermore, *Fallen Angels* carries a dual narrative about two different sets of lovers. The difference is that although *Fallen Angels* can hardly be called a genre film, many of the genre techniques of *As Tears Go By* are back in full force and provide a great deal of the film's energy.

Fallen Angels is set in the Wamchai area of Hong Kong, since Wong felt that he had already "used up" the Tsimshatsui area that had featured so prominently in his previous film (Ngai 85). The city is even more intensely present than it was in *Chungking Express,* especially in the form of zippy montages, exhilarating motorcycle rides, and high-speed time-lapse shots of streaming traffic. It's all superficially exciting but, along with the shabby interiors where hoodlums congregate, ultimately, perhaps, more than a little depressing. (One particularly effective long shot that reappears a number of times shows the pulsating city on the right, with the protagonist in his apartment in the foreground, occupying just a small part of the left hand side of the frame. The difference in scale and dynamism is dizzying.)

The plot is minimal, since the film depends more than ever on violent set pieces, visual effects, and its colorful and even bizarre characters. An assassin (who is called "Ming" in one sequence and is played by Leon Lai) undertakes a series of high-octane group murders under the orders of his beautiful, nameless dispatcher (Michelle Reis). She pines for him, though he rejects any compromising emotional involvement that would extend beyond their professional lives. His character arc, like that of Ah Wah in *As Tears Go By*, leads inevitably toward death.

In the other love story, Ho Chi Moo[16] (Takeshi Kaneshiro) is a mute who lives with his father, who runs a flophouse in Chungking Mansions (site of the first story in *Chungking Express*) where the female dispatcher resides. Owing to his condition, Ho is unable to hold a real job, so he makes a living by breaking into stores (butcher shops, laundries, con-

Figure 8.
Fallen Angels: The
dispatcher (Michelle
Reis) contemplates
her next move.

venience stores, beauty salons, ice cream vans) and forcing passersby to
pay him not, ironically, for any goods he illegally sells them, but to stop
harassing them. He meets and falls in love with Charlie Young,[17] who,
alas, thinks only of the boyfriend who has just jilted her. By the end of
the film, there's a hint that Ho and the dispatcher may be embarking
on a new romance, but only a hint.

Besides the obvious structural and narrative similarities, many of the
tics and tricks that have marked Wong's films heretofore are expressly
repeated here. Characters, locations, and motifs are lifted right out of
Chungking Express: Ho tells us that he became mute when he ate a can
of pineapple that had passed its expiration date, and also that his name is

He Qiwu and that his prison number was 223 (he's played by the same actor who plays officer 223 in *Chungking Express*, Takeshi Kaneshiro). He opines at one point that "we rub shoulders with people every day, strangers who may even have become friends or confidants." A female character obsessively (and clandestinely) cleans the apartment of her blissfully unaware lover while another is supposed to pay an electric bill. And, near the end, a woman dressed as a flight attendant calls her boyfriend from the takeout place Midnight Express. The borrowing, in fact, goes back even further (as for example, when the dispatcher wears a surgical mask while cleaning, like Ngor in *As Tears Go By*), and, once again, voiceover (the communicative vehicle of choice for all four principal characters) carries the primary expository and thematic burden of the film.

All this intra-oeuvre repetition has not sat very well with critics. Howard Hampton has said that "*Fallen Angels* goes off the deep end of self-obsession (it's crammed with so many allusions to his past work, it's like a noisy greatest-hits medley) . . . it's more a frantic résumé than a movie" (92). Ackbar Abbas has also trashed the film: "*Fallen Angels* is once again a reshuffling of elements found in Wong's other films, but in such a way that it verges on being a mere exercise in style. It is indeed a stylish film that runs the risk of being too stylized" (71). Wong, too, has hinted at this problem of repeating oneself when he told Ngai that while it's helpful to work with the same crew all the time, "you have to make double efforts to ensure that you are coming up with new ideas, not just repeating some tried and proven tricks." One way to deal with this, he said, is "to bring in new actors as a stimulant" (112), which is exactly what he did in *Fallen Angels*.

But something about the tenor of this analysis seems shortsighted. While it's true that these familiar motifs lack the resonance with which they are invested elsewhere, precisely because they're familiar, it's almost as though Wong is self-consciously indulging in an orgy of personal intertextuality. Much of his work up to this point has been about the ways that surface can substitute for depth and image can triumph over reality, and in *Fallen Angels* he seems to confront or at least half-confront the implications of this idea more fully, turning his scrutiny on his own work. The films he has already made, in other words, have in turn become part of the vast, unanchored, global image repertoire that can, like everything else, be freely borrowed from. This may not be the wisest aesthetic choice—more about this in a moment—but it nevertheless seems a conscious and purposeful one.

The film is chiefly known for its "experimental" nature: its minimalist plot is especially difficult to follow on a first viewing (as usual, Wong is parsimonious with narrative markers or aids to character recognition), and it revels, even more than its predecessor, in visual style and dramatic fragmentation. The accent, as always, is on visual expressivity—abetted by the aural—through editing (lots of jump cuts), camera movement, and camera angle (a huge number of canted shots) rather than on narrative or theme per se. As Tony Rayns has put it, "scenes turn out to be linked as much by the rhythms of movement and by colour as by theme or motif; what starts out looking like a patchwork turns out to be a fauvist mosaic" ("*Fallen*" 42).

In one expressive but narratively superfluous scene, the dispatcher caresses a Wurlitzer jukebox while the camera caresses her body for an inordinately long time, specifically focusing on the textures of her dress. It's almost as though Wong, through his cinematographer alter ego, Christopher Doyle, were an Old Master painter showing off his ability to render fabric. The gangster genre elements (the film contains five or six separate outbursts of extremely stylized, gun-flashing violence, all of which use Wong's patented stretch-printing process to vary speed), more in evidence than at any time since *As Tears Go By*, seem present both as a commercial calculation and as part of the process of conscious self-quotation described above. During several of the killing scenes, the musical accompaniment to the assassin's work is "Because I'm Cool," a choice that, as in Wong's first film, seems equal parts description and self-parody. Even more than with *As Tears Go By*, it's as though, rather than making a genre film, Wong is making a film about the relation of genre films to art films.

Most impressively—and where it diverges most decisively from *Chungking Express*—the film is shot almost entirely with an extreme wide-angle lens mounted on a handheld camera. Christopher Doyle has explained that prior to *Fallen Angels*, the widest-angle lens that was considered usable was 18 mm, whereas here he used an incredibly wide 6.8 mm lens. "With a 6.8, I can see my assistant standing next to me, it's so wide. The characters have to be very close, because as soon as they get a little further away, they seem too far away. But for this film, for the relation with the characters, the characters among themselves, the existence or the absence of love, it's what was visually necessary" (Niogret, "Entretien" 17). More cryptically, Wong has said that "the reason for using short focal length lenses is that you get a feeling of seeing the characters from a distance even though you're very close to them" (Rayns, "Poet" 13). One other important effect of this choice is that it changes the visual dynamics of one of Wong's favorite shots, the shot that pushes a face toward the viewer in close-up on the left or right side of the frame, while the background of the image shows another figure or figures further away. (The first shot of *Fallen Angels* employs this compositional strategy.) In most of Wong's previous uses of this shot, the background has, owing to focal-length limitations, necessarily been out of focus; here, the extreme wide-angle lens allows everything to be simultaneously sharp, as though Wong had suddenly adopted a Wellesian deep-focus aesthetic. (He hasn't.) The implications for composition and character interaction are extensive. In addition, the distorting effect of the wide-angle lens—which can make even a formidable subway pillar appear momentarily to be a giant, living blob—adds a whole new charge to Wong's visual expressivity.

Adding to this use of the ultra wide-angle lens is the occasional, expressive appearance of black-and-white footage that doesn't ever seem thematically specific to the moment in which it appears, but which endows that moment with a haunting quality nevertheless. Doyle has confessed that five or six reels of spoiled film were accidentally used during the shooting. "So we had the idea of using them in black-and-white and then of rationalizing the idea of using black-and-white" (Niogret, "Entretien" 19). One of most powerful uses of this inadvertent technique comes in a strange, lyrical shot of Ho and Charlie Young, taken through a window in the rain. Bordwell has usefully described this shot in detail in a picture caption in his book: "Dissolving melancholy in *Fallen Angels:* The camera filmed through the bar window while water sprayed onto the window's edges; the actors moved very slowly, the extras in the background moved very fast, and the whole scene was shot at four frames per second. The shot lasts two minutes onscreen, but it took twelve to shoot" (*Planet* 278).

Bordwell proceeds to make a larger point about the meaning of this shot in this film, in Wong's oeuvre overall, and in the larger context of Hong Kong cinema, always an important locus for this critic:

> In *Fallen Angels*, Ho Chi Mo's mooning over Charlie is given a dreamy tentativeness by a more marionettish treatment, enhanced by dripping distortion. For a director interested in memory and ephemerality, variable-speed movement provides an ideal expressive vehicle. Still, the experiment is facilitated by a popular tradition that has routinely slowed or speeded up filming and printing in order to make combat scenes clearer and more forceful. By varying the speed of action, often from shot to shot, Sammo Hung, John Woo, and others provided a norm that Wong could revise for his own ends. (277–78)

Once again, Wong seems to be paradoxically at his most generic when being least so.

Many of Wong's favorite themes and motifs are again present, but in an attenuated form. Western and especially American culture is massively in evidence, as it was in his previous film, but now it takes the specific form of a McDonald's restaurant—significantly, perhaps, it's completely empty except for the two figures the film focuses on—and the ubiquitous English heard on television and radio. More importantly, in this film the Wongian ur-theme of time is never directly thematized and only infrequently represented through the occasional appearance of a clock within the frame. Nevertheless, at crucial moments both male leads say something in voiceover to the effect that "nothing remains the same forever," which of course is the quintessential reference to time. The same obsessive appeal to specific dates ("On May 30, 1995, I fell in love for the first time"; "On August 29, 1995, I ran into my first love again") that we've seen throughout Wong's career reappears, but now primarily for self-referential intertextual or intratextual effect. And though the accent in *Fallen Angels* is on space rather than time, there is one particularly interesting moment where the dispatcher and the assassin occupy the same space—a beauty parlor in which the assassin will later do some serious killing—but not at the same time. Larry Gross has pointed out the "odd temporal effects" that result here: "[Wong] shows the [dispatcher] preceding him through the scene of an assassination, but later he intercuts their movement to condense and smash the logical temporal sequence altogether. He cannot bring them literally together, so the editing process illustrates their proximity, their desire and the impossibility of its fulfillment" (8). Near the end of the film, they do physically meet one last time, and the assassin agrees to a final murder that will get him killed. More interestingly, though, at another point the assassin and the dispatcher "meet" in a very Wongian fashion, by occupying the same seat in the same bar and listening to the same sad song—but at different times.

The characters are by turns cool, vicious, funny, wistful, paranoid, lonely, and childlike. Often the innocent feelings expressed in an endearing voiceover monologue clash violently—and thus humorously—with something atrocious the character has just done. These moments are seldom uproariously funny, and sometimes they seem simply more grotesque than anything else (for example, when Ho, in the butcher shop, sits atop the carcass of a hog and gives it a full-body massage). At other times, the characters seem desperately eager to please and amuse, as when Ho spastically pretends to be a gangster who's just been gunned down (replete with a ketchup-smeared apron) in front of the Midnight Express near the end of the film, to the uncomprehending disapproval of the flight attendant visiting from *Chungking Express*.[18]

Figure 9. *Fallen Angels*: The assassin (Leon Lai) at work.

At still other times, when Ho violently forces innocent late-night visitors to patronize his borrowed businesses—especially the bearded man who has the misfortune to keep running into him—the effect is comic yet uncomfortably invasive at the same time. Abbas offers an interesting political reading of Ho as "not a rebel or a critic of capitalist society. He is merely its negative representation, comically showing how it works non-stop, and its practice of the hard sell" (78). In a similar vein, it's interesting that most of Ho's money comes when people pay him to *stop* trying to sell them things. One specific scene, in which he and Charlie Young beat up a life-size inflatable sex doll, is troubling indeed. After putting a lighted cigarette in its plastic mouth, Ho crushes its head in the elevator. Wong seems to be purposely working a tonal ambiguity here, as a part of a largely covert but nonetheless effective critique of contemporary urban life.

Perhaps the funniest and most endearing moments in *Fallen Angels* rely upon a French New Wave kind of seminonsensical humor reminiscent of films like François Truffaut's *Shoot the Piano Player,* as when Ho tells us, after he commandeers an ice cream van, that his father never drove an ice cream van and still doesn't like ice cream because his mother was killed by one of these vans. Later he opines that as a result of his newfound interest in a girl, his hair is spontaneously turning blonde, perhaps because his mother was Russian. He gratuitously adds that his Chinese father speaks a dialect of Taiwanese that no one else understands, "undoubtedly because of the Russian accent."

Much of the humor, in other words, results from the discrepancy between external reality and a sentiment or interpretation expressed in a character's voiceover. In one scene, however, when the assassin runs into an old high school chum on a bus as he flees the site of a mass murder he has just perpetrated, the humor comes from a simple juxtaposition of character and situation. The assassin's thoroughly middle-class old buddy wants to sell him insurance, and the enormous gap between their chosen professions and lifestyles is, on its own, enough to make you laugh. The assassin never looks directly at the insurance man, who babbles throughout the scene, nor does he say a single word during their bus ride together. This in itself is typical of all the human exchanges in the film, since the actual dialogue spoken directly by one character to another, in the entire film, could probably be reproduced on two pages.

Whatever "encounters" occur—or better, don't occur—do so through voiceover rather than face-to-face interaction.

Sex in this film is more desperate and depressing than ever. As Abbas has put it, "Eroticism in the film is joyless, suspended between boredom and melancholy" (75). Larry Gross's witty comment that "nothing is more typical of the world of Wong Kar-wai than a sex scene where one of the participants isn't present" (10) is never more true than here. One of the saddest moments comes when the dispatcher, clad "erotically" in high heels and fishnet stockings, masturbates alone on the assassin's bed. It's a curiously unerotic shot (from the bottom end of the bed, with the wide-angle lens heavily distorting her legs) that conveys loneliness and isolation more than sensuality. The same thing occurs later in the film, from exactly the same camera angle—we only know it's a different event because the stockings and shoes have changed—suggesting little more than desperation and fruitless repetition. Everyone wants to be noticed here, and the blonde girl in the film (Karen Mok), whose frenetic faux-exuberance often makes her seem on the verge of a nervous breakdown

Figure 10. *Fallen Angels*: The dispatcher (Michelle Reis) amuses herself.

(and which quickly wears thin, until you realize it's supposed to), tells the assassin that she dyed her hair bright blonde "so that no one would forget me."

Musical sound bridges and visual cuts enhance the sexual desperation. As the dispatcher, occupying the assassin's seat in the bar, listens to a coded message he has sent her through the jukebox ("Forget Him"), the music continues over into the assassin's encounter with the blonde girl in McDonald's, suggesting that the same disappointment is in store for her. In her apartment, she tells him that they have been together before, for a long time ("you called me 'baby,'" she chortles), but he doesn't remember and makes it clear to her that he is only interested in a one-night stand. Depressingly, she consoles herself by muttering, "Maybe you'll like me better in the morning." The sound bridge of "Forget Him" then continues its admonitory work by connecting us to the next scene, back on the dispatcher, who is once again masturbating, which is followed by a lengthy period of sobbing. Not a very hopeful picture of heterosexual relationships, certainly, yet its implications extend even further, since desperate sex is only a sign of a more generalized loneliness. At one point, Ho considers making videotapes to send as greetings, as his friend Sato-san does to his son, but decides against it: "Who would I send tapes to? I really can't send them to myself." This echoes the assassin's reason for deciding against taking out an insurance policy: "Who would I name as the beneficiary?" As Tony Rayns has succinctly put it, "Loneliness is ultimately the film's centrifugal force" ("*Fallen*" 42). All that was frothy and fun in *Chungking Express* has now, very purposely, I think, become pathetic and alienated.

By the last sequence of the film, virtually every possible amorous combination has been worked through. It ends with a lovely sequence in which Ho and the dispatcher have been left alone in a restaurant, following a fight in which Ho has participated. In voice-over, we have just heard from each one seemingly innocent comments about the weather that obviously contain other meanings as well. Ho says: "I hadn't expected winter to come so soon." And she: "I feel cold." Both speak of being "more careful" now, solely, yet again, in voice-over. Still in the restaurant, we then hear from each why nothing can happen between them. Ho's comment is particularly funny, because he is speaking of being an eternal optimist while soaked in his own blood from the fight.

Figure 11. *Fallen Angels*: A happy ending? The dispatcher (Michelle Reis) and Ho/He (Takeshi Kaneshiro) on his motorcycle.

Yet he tells us, "Maybe it was the weather, but that night I found her very alluring." And suddenly they are off together on his motorcycle, streaming through the cross-harbor tunnel that we've seen several times before. The close-up of her head on his shoulder is heartrendingly gorgeous, perhaps the most powerful single shot in the whole film. As she speaks the final voice-over, the shot gradually widens to include Ho as well: "I haven't been this close to a man in ages," she confides to us. "The road home isn't very long. And I know I'll be getting off soon. But at this moment I'm feeling such lovely warmth." This sentiment remains locked up in voice-over and, heaven forbid, is not expressed directly to this other present human being in actual dialogue, but it's a tiny sign of a hopeful, connected future. Which is about all the optimism this brilliantly downbeat, thoroughly depressed movie can muster. In this light, Wong's comment to Tony Rayns that *Fallen Angels* "is all about ways to keep yourself happy" can only be seen as bitterly ironic ("Poet" 14).

The two most interesting things about *Fallen Angels* that remain to be discussed concern a view of love that hasn't been expressed thus far in Wong's oeuvre and the placement of the director himself autobiographically into one of the characters. Regarding the first, Ho decides in the middle of the film to take up a video camera to document his father's life. Though his father pretends to resist, Ho discovers to his delight that his father gets up at night to watch his image on the screen, an activity that obviously makes him happy. When his father dies, Ho turns to this video image for solace in a powerfully moving way, a moment of real, pure love—though, once again, only manifested through absence—that is virtually unheard of in a Wong film. Ho tells us that now that his father is gone, he feels grown-up for the first time. Then, devastatingly, he quietly adds: "I didn't want to be grown-up, I just wanted Dad with me." Though this relationship is nonsexual, and though we never see it overtly expressed, it is much more affecting than anything else in the amorously frustrating world that Wong's characters inhabit. It is a real love if, once again, only expressible in the context of its loss and its impossibility. Time, that other great Wongian theme, is foregrounded when Ho plays the videotapes over and over, speeding them up, slowing them down, figuratively mastering time through its artistic representation (with the aid of the rewind button) and thus also mastering his father's death in a way that he cannot in reality.

The second especially interesting thing about this film is the manner in which Wong inserts himself so directly into the film text through his stand-in, the wannabe video/filmmaker Ho. (Ho even tells us at one point that he emigrated to Hong Kong at the age of five—just as Wong did—though in Ho's case it was from Taiwan, not Shanghai.) This connection between them is signaled even more strongly because, in one of the few overtly Brechtian moments in Wong's films, Ho directly addresses us during his voiceover, making eye contact, as though Ho were *himself* shooting the part of the film in which he is featured. Chuck Stephens has offered an imaginative and convincing interpretation of this relationship, seeing in it a reference to Wong's conflicted place in the Hong Kong film industry:

> The use to which [Wong] puts his apparent alter ego, Kaneshiro [the actor who plays Ho] . . . blurs beyond self-parody into a wisecracking mode of mock-autobiography. In a funhouse reflection of Wong's jockeying for position both within and without Hong Kong's generic corral, Kaneshiro's mute—who nevertheless babbles endlessly in voiceover—

spends his time breaking into other folks' businesses during the night, eking out what little living he can by coercing passersby into becoming his reluctant customers. (18)

Wong's own take on what he thought he was doing in this film is somewhat surprising, but only at first glance. "For me," he told Michel Ciment and Hubert Niogret, "*Fallen Angels* was like a comic book, with four completely one-dimensional principal characters. The only real character, in the strong sense of the term, was the father of one of the young people. In this sense, the film reflects the enormous influence of the comics on Hong Kong cinema. The audience can then compare real characters with the comic book heroes. The experience of *Happy Together* [Wong's next film] is of course very different. . . . [I]t's a simple, direct film about normal people" (Ciment and Niogret, "Entretien" [1997] 13). Wong demonstrates again how close his films remain to the popular culture that is the source of what is best in Hong Kong cinema. I would argue, however, that it's precisely in these challenging, unexpected *juxtapositions*—in this particular film, for example, of the real and the cartoonlike—that the nongeneric specialness, the artistry of Wong's films, appears.

The director's characterization of *Happy Together* as "a simple, direct film about normal people" is clearly meant as a joke, as we shall see in the next section. There's no doubt that this next film is very different from what has gone before, but not in the way that Wong would have us believe. Having reached the depths of urban alienation and self-quoting self-indulgence in the brilliant but perhaps ultimately too-cold *Fallen Angels,* Wong is now ready to move beyond anomie and back to love and—this will never change—the multiple and apparently inescapable frustrations that attend it.

Happy Together

With *Happy Together* and *In the Mood for Love,* Wong Kar-wai reaches the zenith of his cinematic art. The endearing and often exuberant visual and aural effects are still much in evidence, but in a gratifyingly lower key. We are stimulated at regular intervals by the amazing formal

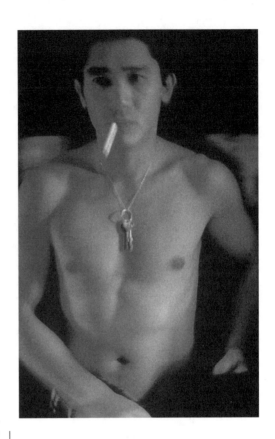

Figure 12. *Happy
Together:* Lai Yiu-fai
(Tony Leung Chiu-wai)
shows his stuff.

energy of these techniques, but now, restrained, they no longer occupy
center stage.

His previous two films clearly indicate a potentially new direction
for the cinema of the future, a novel graphic and aural expressivity that
makes most other contemporary films seem pale and lifeless by comparison. I also believe that *Fallen Angels* has hidden depths that most
critics have missed. Nevertheless, it seems that a more mature Wong
has come to realize, in his two most recent films, that the controlling

aesthetic of his earlier work—ebullient style sometimes indulged for its own sake—has its limitations. *Happy Together*[19] is a powerful, haunting work, but these qualities more clearly emanate from the characters and their situation—"plot" is probably too strong a word to use for this film, where little actually happens—rather than the stimulus of a hyperactive technique itself.

As originally conceived, the story, based loosely on a novel by Manuel Puig called *An Affair in Buenos Aires,* concerned a man who travels to Buenos Aires to investigate his father's murder and in the process discovers that he had a gay lover there. Wong says, however, that he quickly realized that the novel contained too many different stories to handle adequately, including the investigation, the problems of the son in Hong Kong, the life of his father, the father's relations with his lover ten years earlier, and so on. Besides, the production was beset with difficulties: Wong's veteran star, the late Leslie Cheung, who plays one of the two central characters in the film, was also scheduled to return to Hong Kong for a concert, hence they only had a month to shoot (in fact, the shooting went on for four months); there was a strike; and they were cheated by a local production company. "Time was flying by and I decided to make the simplest possible story, a road movie, once again, with a new encounter between these two men who come from Hong Kong and end up in Buenos Aires without knowing why" (Ciment and Niogret, "Entretien" [1997] 9).

The plot of the finished film, as usual, is supremely minimal and, since it proceeds mostly on the basis of looks and gestures, difficult to summarize. Two Hong Kong men, Lai Yiu-fai (Tony Leung Chiu-wai) and Ho Po-wing (Leslie Cheung), homosexual lovers who have been struggling through a difficult relationship for some time, travel to Buenos Aires for reasons that are never made entirely clear. Yiu-fai, who works as a greeter at a tango club, wants to return to Hong Kong, but he has no money. Po-wing, who, to the annoyance of Yiu-fai, supports himself through prostitution, is often beaten up. The chronological lines of the film are never very clear, but the lovers seem to alternate between being unhappily together and being unhappily apart. They plan to go to the famous Iguazu Falls together, in Brazil, but they never make it. Yiu-fai, who bitterly rejects Po-wing's recurrent suggestion to "start over again," reluctantly decides to care for his lover when he is severely beaten. As

Po-wing's health improves, they jog, go to the racetrack, and practice tango steps; eventually, against his better judgment, Yiu-fai once again becomes emotionally involved. He takes a job in a restaurant, where he meets another young man, Chang (Chen Chang), also from Hong Kong, who is especially gifted in the perception of sounds. To make enough money to return to Hong Kong as soon as possible, Yiu-fai takes a job in a slaughterhouse and finally reveals that he had left Hong Kong because he dishonored his father by stealing some money. At the end of the film, Chang visits the southernmost point of South America, Yiu-fai visits the Iguazu Falls alone, and a lonely Po-wing sobs bitterly in Yiu-fai's former apartment. We last see Yiu-fai in Taiwan—where he visits the food stall of Chang's family—on his way back home to Hong Kong to make amends with his father, presumably, and to live the rest of his life.

Unlike Wong's earlier films, the narrative focuses relentlessly on a single couple. Only when a third party, Chang, is introduced two-thirds of the way through the film do we realize how all-consuming Wong's concentration on Po-wing and Yiu-fai has been. The purposeful doubling effected by parallel narratives is now gone, along with the overt interrogation of subjectivity, but in their place has come a new and welcome intensification of our emotional relationship with these two people. This intensity is enhanced by the fact that, though one might expect a clash of languages and cultures in a movie about two Chinese men in Argentina, the clash never really occurs. Instead, while Spanish is the context of all that we see and hear, at least in principle, it remains in the background, utterly alien to the bizarre, totalizing core of Chinese language and culture that exclusively holds center stage and forms a kind of inviolable otherness in the heart of Buenos Aires. Wong told *Positif* that "it was if I had reconstituted Hong Kong in Buenos Aires. . . . [A]t the beginning, I tried to understand Buenos Aires and its inhabitants. But I quickly realized that I didn't have the time to open myself up" (Ciment and Niogret, "Entretien" [1997] 8–9).

In more functional narrative terms, the film is, like all of Wong's films, often difficult to follow. The viewer must pay close attention, as scenes are often explained only after they take place (as when we watch the lovers haphazardly running along a bridge in an extended sequence, for no apparent reason, then find out in the next scene that they had been jogging). Wong relies once again on voice-over, but in this film its role is somewhat reduced, more conventionally, to providing minimal exposition, as well as the intimate calibration of Yiu-fai's feelings.[20] In the earlier films, the very existence of so much voice-over was a sign of the characters' alienation from one another, but *Happy Together* actually contains a great deal of dialogue. The alienation remains, but it's shown through the more conventional—and perhaps more emotionally involving—method of having characters talk to (and scream at) each other. And though the result is hardly a ringing endorsement of the redeeming power of love, it seems that, for once, the characters, even if they're arguing, at least directly engage each other. The alienation now comes, in other words, from too much emotion rather than not enough.

The narrative is enriched once again by various literary-style motifs. The waterfall that the couple unsuccessfully attempts to visit in the beginning of the film and which Yiu-fai, all alone, reaches at the end bears the film's principal symbolic burden. As a natural phenomenon, it is spectacularly beautiful—especially as shot by Christopher Doyle, in a single take, hanging out of a tilted helicopter circling around the falls. It is seen near the beginning of the film and repeated near the end. Symbolically, it seems to represent a utopian point of pure idealization, forever unreachable in the real world, something like an unencumbered love between two human beings. Since it is also figured on the lampshade in Yiu-fai's apartment, an interesting, deeply resonant doubling of representation takes place. Wong told *Positif* that when he and the crew were trying to furnish Yiu-fai's apartment, they found twin lamps with the waterfall shade. "And, in looking at the picture, I saw two little men looking at the waterfall. That seemed like a beautiful story to include in my film: this idea of a man who would like to share his happiness with another by going to see the waterfall. That gave them a common goal and also helped us structure the story" (Ciment and Niogret, "Entretien" [1997] 9).

Another curious motif is the whimsical prioritization of hearing over sight, especially as embodied in the secondary character Chang. This new friend of Yiu-fai, who has an inordinately sharp sense of hearing, tells him in the bar they frequent, the Tres Amigos (a purposely symbolic—or tongue-in-cheek—name?), that "you can see better with your ears. You can pretend to be happy, but your voice can't lie." In a later scene in the bar, when Chang tells Yiu-fai that he is leaving for the "end of the world" at the southern tip of South America, Yiu-fai tells him that he's heard that "people with emotional problems can dump all their troubles there." Chang then asks Yiu-fai if he will record his voice for him, as a souvenir of their friendship, rather than posing for the more conventional photograph. Yiu-fai, who has just insisted to Chang that he isn't unhappy, can, however, do little more than sob into the recorder.

Perhaps because the handover of Hong Kong to the Chinese authorities was about to become a reality at the time the film was made, identity, specifically the narrow political identity that is linked to nation and legality, is important in *Happy Together* to a greater extent than in earlier films. The opening shot is of Yiu-fai's and Po-wing's passports, which establishes who they (legally) are, even before we see the title of the film. Sheldon Hsiao-peng Lu has pointed out that though the passports say "British nationality," "Hong Kong residents were granted the right to free travel to most countries by the British administration, yet most of them were not allowed to become permanent residents of Great Britain" ("Filming" 280). Stokes and Hoover develop this theme by claiming that the title that follows the shot of the passports is a "statement" because it is "colored in the red and white of the Hong Kong flag" (268).

In this same vein, Lu perhaps overreads—though provocatively—a later detail concerning Liaoning Street, the market street in Taipei (Taiwan) that Yiu-fai walks down at the end of the film. Since it is also the name of a province on the Chinese mainland, Lu claims that it "is thus a mapping of the geopolitical imaginary of the Chinese nation as the Republic of China in Taiwan proclaims to be the only legitimate sovereign Chinese state. In such a manner, the street sign points to both the unity of the Chinese nation and its fragmentation. The evocation of such a fragmented collective further heightens the sense of displacement of ethnic Chinese across the mainland, Taiwan, Hong Kong, and the various continents" ("Filming" 280). More convincing is Lu's emphasis on the news report of the death of Deng Xiaopeng that Yiu-fai sees on TV in his Taipei hotel room, since Deng was the architect of a plan to reunite mainland China and Taiwan under the Hong Kong "one country, two systems" model. In any case, Lu's suggestion regarding this scene—that "however displaced and scattered on the edge of the world, the migrant Hong Konger is nonetheless linked to China in real or imagined space and time" (281)—rings true. He concludes that "the film does not end on a pessimistic, apocalyptic note of impending doom in view of Hong Kong's return to China but with the possibility of a new beginning. At least it is safe to say that the ending is more ambiguous than negative" (282).

Stokes and Hoover unabashedly call *Happy Together* "Wong's most direct political statement to date—a challenge to the 'normalization' of Hong Kong–Mainland relations on the eve of the handover," mostly owing to the gay subject matter, which "transgressed mainstream Chinese standards" (268). Given the film's audacious representation of homosexuality, this reading seems quite plausible. Their conclusion is somewhat more negative than Lu's: "*Happy Together* offers several possible scenarios for the reunion of Hong Kong and China: escape, lament, embrace, acceptance, and choice. Rather than provide simple commentary, the movie maps out complications, contradictions, and conflicts, reflecting the preoccupations and concerns of Hong Kong people on the brink of the handover" (278).

The political readings these critics offer can be convincing, but in their totalizing effect, they seem to disallow the possibility that these films are about love and personal happiness as well. (It should be noted in passing that Wong told *Positif* that after *Fallen Angels,* everyone was asking him if he was going to make a film on the handover. "Since I didn't know what to respond, the best way of avoiding the question was to go shoot elsewhere" [Ciment and Niogret, "Entretien" (1997) 8].) Whatever the political complexities of the film, in other words, Wong clearly remains interested in his typical theme of love and its sundry permutations. For one thing, the film begins with a provocative, no-holds-barred homosexual love scene, as though to establish immediately the physical nature of the men's relationship, perhaps shock the viewer (and maybe the censors in mainland China, as Stokes and Hoover suggest), and then get it out of the way.[21] Yet it's also true that kissing and some less overt moments of physical intimacy take place throughout the film, especially when they dance, so the idea promulgated by Wong in interviews—that if a viewer came in late and missed the opening sex scene, he or she could easily think the film was about two brothers—is completely misleading and presumably meant as a joke. To Wong's credit, Po-wing's need for sex is never condemned and is never represented as something inherently "homosexual." Nor, happily, is their constant bickering so portrayed.

However, a debate has arisen among critics concerning the extent to which this can be labeled a "homosexual" film. Each side has cited contradictory statements Wong has made in different interviews to bolster its arguments. Of the opening scene, Wong has said, "I treated it in a very direct, very explicit fashion in order to show that that was part of their life, like having a meal together or washing their clothes. . . . Once the film was finished, I realized that it was simply a love story" (Ciment and Niogret, "Entretien" [1997] 8). It's always in a director's interest, of course, for his film to be understood in the widest possible context. But speaking to Bérénice Reynaud, Wong seems to indicate that it was the specific nature of their sexual relationship that interested him the most: "The few Hong Kong films which treat homosexuality do it comically, and I wanted to approach the subject without making people laugh. For me, homosexuality, like Argentina, is the other end of the world, and thus a particularly interesting subject" ("*Happy*" 76).

A fresh approach to the subject is taken by Marc Siegel in "The Intimate Spaces of Wong Kar-Wai," which counters the conventional view of Wong's films, especially *Happy Together*, as lamentations over the alienation and loneliness of contemporary life. Siegel insists that "Wong's films challenge the idea that intimacy can be confined within the form of the couple and within the realm of the private" (286). In his view, Wong explores the changes that have accompanied globalization and works to break down the distinction between public and private: "Wong's images are only disappointments to those who expect the affective relations between the characters to remain the same in a world of spatial and temporal disjuncture. If globalism generates the possibilities for new kinds of looking, does it not also offer the potential for new kinds of feeling, new kinds of intimacy?" (288). As an example, Siegel offers Chang's great listening ability: "Able to hear conversations from across a crowded bar, Chang experiences intimacy independently of both proximity and reciprocity" (290). But can intimacy be achieved if the other remains completely unaware? Is this what we mean by intimacy?

In any case, while not wanting to take away from the homosexual specificity of the film—and thus perhaps rob it of another kind of political force—it's easy to see it as another film about the frustrating impossibility of all love, not only the homosexual variety. The motif of "starting over," for example—ever hopeful and yet pathetically self-deluding at the same time—will be familiar to some viewers of all sexual preferences. Interestingly, by the end of the film Yiu-fai invokes the phrase "starting over" for his relationship with his father. It's as though Ho's feelings toward his father had carried over from *Fallen Angels,* and it indicates that the most seemingly different varieties of love are perhaps all of a piece.

As always, Wong's themes are instantiated in a blinding array of cinematic techniques. Color plays a somber but richly expressionistic role that it hasn't since Wong's earliest films, such as *As Tears Go By* and *Days of Being Wild.* A powerfully haunting shot will suddenly appear—for example, of the couple in the back seat of a taxi, on the drive from the hospital—that achieves much of its effect through its deep brown hue, with Po-wing's bandaged hands plaintively and uselessly extended in front of him. Wong is smart enough to let Po-wing's touch-

Figure 13. *Happy Together.* Back from the hospital by taxi, Yiu-fai (Tony Leung Chiu-wai, right) isn't convinced about Ho Po-wing's (Leslie Cheung) fidelity.

ing gesture—gently laying his head on Yiu-fai's shoulder—carry the moment, without the assistance of superfluous dialogue. The romantic Spanish music does the rest.

Black-and-white film stock is also used expressively throughout the film, as when Yiu-fai confesses poignantly in voice-over that he didn't want Po-wing to recover too quickly from his injuries because these were in fact their happiest days together. Here the footage resembles nothing so much as a badly exposed, jump-cut-marred home movie that serves as the counterpart to Yiu-fai's voice-over monologue, the visual version of the memory that is being expressed orally. Occasionally, the color stock is difficult to distinguish from the black-and-white when it yields an impression of the monochromatic tinting associated with silent films. (Thus, the drenched red of evening, or in front of the tango bar where Yiu-fai parks cars, or when Yiu-fai and Chang have a beer; or the deep blue associated with the waterfall and the cold bridge on which Po-wing and Yiu-fai go jogging; or the yellow that saturates the apartment, when Yiu-fai is in a rage.) The black-and-white stock, Wong pointed out to an interviewer, was used to capture the cold months in Argentina as well to set the film's chronology, though the experience of watching the film yields a timeline much less precise than the one Wong outlines here:

> I love the texture [of black-and-white film]. I also wanted to separate the film into three parts. For the audience, the past is often associated with black-and-white. The second part is when the two men decide to start living together again. And the third is when Po-wing leaves Tony. The story becomes more interior then. They don't see each other any longer, nor do they talk to anyone else, just themselves. I remembered the first sentence of Godard's *Le petit soldat:* "For me, the time for action has passed. I've gotten older. The time for reflection now begins." And this is a little what happened in the third part of the film. (Ciment and Niogret, "Entretien" [1997] 14)

A time-lapse shot of a monumental street in Buenos Aires, used twice, recalls the wildly streaming cars in Hong Kong from Wong's earlier movies, though for an American the most immediate (and uncanny) association for the shot, which contains a tall white obelisk in the center of the image, is the Washington Monument. Discreetly to the side is a digital clock, which recalls Wong's obsession with time and whose hypercharged numbers (owing to the time-lapse photography) call attention to the stylized expressiveness of the shot. According to Wong, this shot was also designed to contrast with Yiu-fai's apartment: "In this room and in their existence, there's no progression. There's a very routine side of their life, whereas outside the world never stops moving" (Ciment and Niogret, "Entretien" [1997] 14). This contrast is extended during certain sequences, especially the three times that a soccer game is being played in the alley, in which the handheld camera is shooting into the sun, and the viewer can barely make out who's playing. Moments of intense vitality like this offer a sharp contrast, visually and thematically, to the brooding, purposely inert quality of the rest of the film. This juxtaposition is also occasionally achieved through the sudden infusion of a intense primary color into the image, as when the bright red of the (tomato?) sauce in Yiu-fai's kitchen—echoed later by the swirling blood of the slaughterhouse where he works—bursts suddenly before our dazzled eyes.

Although its visual track is more restrained than the inspired mayhem of *Chungking Express* and *Fallen Angels,* one of the most fascinating aspects of *Happy Together* is that Wong employs a greater and richer panoply of formal devices than in his earlier work. The experience of watching the film resembles nothing so much as that of watching a European art film from the 1960s (especially the opening scenes, in black-and-white). For one thing, Wong is not above cracking a visual joke in the style of the French New Wave, as in *Fallen Angels.* Near the end of *Happy Together,* for example, when Yiu-fai says that from his perspective in Buenos Aires, Hong Kong must be upside-down, we get a breezy montage of tall Hong Kong buildings seen upside-down. On a more serious level, Wong brilliantly uses mise-en-scène to express emotion, as when he has the two protagonists sit in different seats on the bus, one behind the other, so that they can't see each other's faces, emphasizing their individual isolation. (This is a more classical variant on the wide-angle lens used in *Fallen Angels,* which often achieves the same effect.)

Camera position is often deliberately thematic, foregrounding an inanimate object front and center, for example, while decentering the characters and pushing them to the margins (think of the camera's odd focus on a car headlight in beginning of the film, when the couple is trying to find the waterfall, or, in Yiu-fai's apartment, the end of the sofa that occupies so much of the image, while Yiu-fai is jammed way over to its left). Camera distance, likewise, is often used for expressive purposes, and we sometimes jump from a jerky handheld shot to a fixed, extreme long shot that allows the rest of the frame to achieve an expressive purpose through its composition. At other moments—when Po-wing returns following Yiu-fai's anxious search for him, or when Po-wing searches for his passport, which Yiu-fai has hidden, and they fight—Wong unleashes a brief but powerful combination of wide-angle shots, violent character movements, and sharp, ultra-quick jump cuts that grabs our attention and marks the moment indelibly.

One memorable shot in the apartment, in which Po-wing suddenly and inexplicably disappears, is well described by Stokes and Hoover: "One filmic image resonates with Po-wing's characterization. Seated in their room at the table, Po-wing is glimpsed in a medium shot. He looks outside the balcony doors as a breeze gently blows the translucent curtains. One moment he is there, the next he is gone, while the rest of the shot remains the same. He is a ghost of a character, registered by his absence, his inability to commit to a relationship, and his confusion and pain" (275).

And though Wong's technical panoply is more restrained (if more ample) in this film, he has hardly foresworn the innovative techniques that have served him so well. Thus, the familiar stretch-printing method reappears, but here, for once, it's not in the service of a gunfight. Instead, it captures Yiu-fai frantically searching for Po-wing, and its expressive effect is powerful because we care for this character more than for Wong's previous characters. At other times, Wong only slightly slows everything down for a few fleeting moments, merely to achieve the added expressivity of a softly curling wisp of cigarette smoke. To my mind, at least, this occasional slight retardation of the image, or the minor jump-cut effect provided by extremely brief freeze-frames (for example, when he says goodbye to Chang, indicating some emotional connection between them), provides infinitely more expressive nuance than any close-up of a face could offer.

We are fortunate to have the diary that Wong's celebrated cinematographer, Christopher Doyle, kept during the shooting of the film, and it deserves to be quoted at length. Here's his take on the film's visual strategies:

At first we hesitated to repeat our "signature style," but eventually it was just too frustrating not to. We do more and more in-shot speed changes as the film goes on. From "normal" speed to 12 or eight frames-per-second—or the other way around. And our notionally taboo wide-angle lenses are being brought in more and more often, to make a "flat" image more "interesting." I've always associated our "blurred action" sequences with the adrenaline rush triggered by fear or violence. This time around it's more "druggy." We change speed at "decisive," "ephi-phanal," or "revelatory" moments. The actor moves extremely slowly while all else goes on in "real time." The idea is to suspend time, to emphasise and prolong the "relevance" of whatever is going on. This is, I'm told, what a hit of heroin is like. The bitch, for the actors, is how fast or slow to talk. (16)

In an interview with *Positif*, Doyle gave an illuminating example of the sometimes fortuitous relation of form and content that can occur on a Wong Kar-wai set:

One day, on *Happy Together*, we were shooting in the bedroom. We were getting ready to go to lunch. The camera was stuck under the bed without unplugging the monitor, and suddenly we discovered an angle that we had never thought of, even though we had been shooting on that set for two days. So we decided to use that angle. It had a feeling of loneliness and malaise. And that's the kind of feeling we were shooting that day. The people on the team were open to whatever might happen. Life isn't something continuous and coherent. You shouldn't standardize things. (Niogret, "Entretien" 17).

As always in Wong's films, the effect of the striking visuals is invari-ably enhanced by the sounds and especially the music employed. The powerfully romantic effect that was achieved through the use of the Hawaiian guitar in *Days of Being Wild* now finds expression through an equally romantic strain of Spanish music (here the tango), a variant of which will be utilized again in *In the Mood for Love*. The particular tango music that appears in *Happy Together*—abetted at crucial moments by the well-known pop song by the Turtles—is a variety called the "new tango," developed by the Argentinian musician Astor Piazzolla. Wong claims that he didn't know Piazzolla's work until he bought a CD in the Amsterdam airport on the way to Buenos Aires, but that it ultimately gave him "the rhythm of the film and that of the town in which it was made" (Ciment and Niogret, "Entretien" [1997] 10).

These manifold techniques serve a striking story line that, while sketchy and sometimes difficult to discern, remains powerful and direct, rising to a gradual crescendo from the midpoint on. When Po-wing arrives at his apartment after being severely beaten, love, however it might be defined, induces Yiu-fai to take him back despite his powerful reluctance to do so. On Po-wing's release from the hospital, Yiu-fai lovingly feeds and bathes him, and much later in the film, he confides to us in voiceover that this was the happiest moment in their relationship. It's a heartbreaking claim, because it implies that only when the other is incapacitated, and therefore less than a full, autonomous self, can unmitigated love ever truly flourish. They try jogging on the cold bridge one day, and when Yiu-fai gets sick, Po-wing genuinely attempts to take care of him but fails, since it's just not in his nature. Yiu-fai cooks, despite his illness—as always in a Wong film, food is associated with love—they go to the racetrack, they practice the tango in a gorgeously

Figure 14. *Happy Together.* A lovely moment between Yiu-fai (Tony Leung Chiu-wai) and Po-wing (Leslie Cheung), practicing the tango in their kitchen.

romantic sequence, and as Po-wing gets stronger daily, the viewer knows that something surely will go wrong.

Both lovers are wracked by jealousy and the resultant issues of control, and they bitterly accuse each other of infidelity. Near the end, when they seem to have separated for good, each turns to the frantic, anonymous sex of the public lavatory and the porn theater. Yiu-fai tells us in voice-over, "I thought I was different from Po-wing, [but it] turns out that lonely people are all the same." It is only at this moment that we discover that Yiu-fai originally traveled to Argentina because of his estrangement with his father over some money Yiu-fai had stolen. (In a fantasized Hollywood version of this story, one can imagine that this fact would have been Yiu-fai's single motivating factor, revealed as early as possible.)

On his way back to Hong Kong, Yiu-fai visits the glorious waterfall that he and Po-wing never succeeded in reaching. (This idea of a spiritually fulfilling quest to an exotic location, repeated and expanded from *Days of Being Wild*, will appear again at the end of *In the Mood for Love*.) We cut to Po-wing slow-dancing the tango with another man, a sequence that is devastatingly intercut with shots of Po-wing and Yiu-fai dancing together in happier times, to a richly romantic score. We then see Po-wing sitting on the steps of the tango bar where Yiu-fai worked; he's all splayed out, the position of his body speaking volumes, but the shot is accompanied by no additional narrative explanation. Wong's expression of the tragic impossibility of love reaches its apogee here in a moment of powerful intercutting: As Po-wing sobs bitterly on their old bed, while looking at the souvenir lamp of the falls, we see Yiu-fai standing on a bridge near the real falls, the cleansing water pouring over him, as he tells us in voice-over: "There should be two of us standing here."[22]

The camera, in a supremely expressive helicopter shot that is the emotional high point of the film, circles around the falls. Lovely music plays (Caetano Veloso singing "Cucurrucucu Paloma" and Astor Piazzolla doing "Tango Apasionado [Finale]") while the visual track is pervaded by a deep blue. The song finally fades, and for a long time all that we hear is the music of the roaring water. The effect is enormously haunting. We cut to Chang on his lighthouse at the end of the world, as the camera lyrically circles him in a movement that parallels the circling of the falls. It is January 1997, and he tells us, "I promised Fai to leave his sadness here." He listens to Yiu-fai's tape and tells us that, surprisingly, there is nothing on it besides a strange noise that sounds like someone sobbing.

Chang returns to Buenos Aires on his way back to Taipei, in hopes of finding Yiu-fai at the Tres Amigos. He's not there, and when Chang tries to catch a trace of his voice by means of his hypersensitive hearing, he can't hear it, he says, because the music is too loud. We then see Yiu-fai in Taipei, on his way back to Hong Kong. A quick shot of the television news in his hotel room tells us that Deng Xiaopeng has died, which will mean a new (though not necessarily better) future for China and, by extension, for Chinese people everywhere.

Yiu-fai walks through the market toward Chang's family's hawker stall that Chang himself has reluctantly decided to return to. The vitality of the place, like the soccer games in Buenos Aires, appears to lift Yiu-fai's spirits. Wong plays with the viewer here, for at first we think that he doesn't know this is Chang's family's stall—Chang isn't there at the moment—and Wong even goes so far as to show us pictures of Chang at the lighthouse, stuck on the wall, pictures that Yiu-fai apparently can't see. So close but so far, we worry. Then Yiu-fai relieves us by saying that he now knows where to find Chang, then steals a photo of him; by this means, Wong avoids the sentimentality of a happy ending yet manages to leave us at least a shred of hope that Yiu-fai may someday find happiness.

So much motion, so little progress. Abbas nicely links these characters' movements through space with their emotions: "In *Happy Together*, then, even more centrally than in Wong's other films, spatial experiences parallel and counterpoint affective experience, the nomadic and the erotic arrive at similar conclusions. . . . If the search for happiness is, as we are suggesting, like looking for the end of the world, i.e., an impossibility, yet in the film, the characters continue to do both in spite of repeated disappointments" (81).

Finally, we cut to a bright subway slashing its way through Taipei, with the Turtles' theme song at full volume in the background. We see time-lapse shots of thousands of people running through shopping malls, and we are impressed by all this vitality. We discover Yiu-fai on the subway. He looks pensive, and then, in a maddeningly ambiguous moment, he appears to take something out of his pocket and look at it for just a second—we can only surmise that this is what he is doing, since the shot only shows his face—and a tiny smile appears. Has he looked at the photo of Chang? As the subway train hurtles into the bright white station, freeze-frame. The End. The Turtles song continues, however, and we suddenly realize that Yiu-fai is still in love with Po-wing and probably always will be. The lyrics spell it loud and clear: "I can't see me lovin' nobody but you for all my life." But maybe Stokes and Hoover say it best: "Fai learns to get over Po-wing and on with his life. He doesn't stop loving Po-wing, just as he doesn't choose to love him to begin with, but he makes a choice about how to love him, where they can be 'happy together'—at a distance" (272).[23] And then again—though no other critic, to my knowledge, has mentioned this, and it may well be a figment of my imagination—there is also the possibility of Chang.

The last word should be left to a surprisingly upbeat Christopher Doyle: "It's our brightest film in all senses of the word and looks like having the happiest ending of any WKW film. It's also much more 'coherent' than our other films, and very lyrical. Of course the traditional WKW themes of 'time' and 'loss' put in appearances. And there are plenty of great lines, my favourite being: 'Starting over means heading for one more break-up'" (17).

In the Mood for Love

With *In the Mood for Love*,[24] his most recent and perhaps greatest film, Wong Kar-wai makes multiple returns while nevertheless proceeding in completely new directions. In terms of setting, we are back in the historically re-created Hong Kong of the 1960s last seen in *Days of Being Wild,* but now, as Wong has stressed in interviews, we are dealing with mature married people. (In other words, people who resemble the director as he is now, just as the characters in *Days* resembled him then.) He has also said that the earlier film was "a very personal reinvention of the '60s," but in the new film "we consciously tried to re-create the actuality. I wanted to say something about daily life then" (Rayns, "In the Mood" 17).[25]

The heterosexual couple has returned to center stage, displacing the homosexual pairing of *Happy Together* (but Wong has said that the latter was a movie about a love affair, rather than a gay movie, so perhaps the displacement is not so great after all). In this film, which took fifteen

Figure 15. *In the Mood for Love*: Su Li-zhen (Maggie Cheung) and Chow Mo-wan (Tony Leung Chiu-wai) observe the social proprieties.

grueling months to make—a period during which the actors Tony Leung and Maggie Cheung were, by all accounts, including theirs, driven to the point of desperation—visual and aural techniques continue to be used, brilliantly, for their expressive richness. Yet, as in Wong's previous movie, form remains resolutely in the service of character, theme, and emotion rather than indulged for its own sake.

What is noticeably different is the social context within which the individual love story takes place. In *Happy Together*, the Argentinian environment of the Chinese lovers was barely hinted at, remaining little more than a minimal backdrop, an exotic otherness whose shadowy presence served primarily to intensify the film's central focus. Now, however, the lovers or, rather, potential lovers—one of the sublime frustrations of the film is that they never actually become lovers in the physical sense[26]—are always seen within a cramped social field. This psychologically and physically constrained environment will rule their lives and, by keeping them from acting on their justified impulses, stunt their happiness forever.

At first glance this context seems warm and nurturing, partly because it is so deeply related to Wong's own childhood memories of this time and place, as a five-year-old immigrant to Hong Kong from Shanghai. But this illusion is quickly dispelled. The stifling conformity and hypocrisy of this society is everywhere evident, perhaps most emblematically in the decision of a middle-class shipping executive, Mr. Ho, that his new tie is too "showy," though he is going out on a date with his mistress and apparently has no qualms about cheating on his wife. Narratively speaking, the most profound (and most logical) consequence of this decision to emphasize social context is that for the first time in a Wong film there is no formal voiceover, since the individual is now downplayed. Despite this new focus on the social collectivity, however, Wong has hardly forsaken his interest in exploring the nature of subjectivity.

The film begins with a dynamic composition of bold red and white titles, accompanied by complete silence. The poetic intertitle that follows, while respecting the power disparity that inheres in all gender difference, nevertheless emphasizes the possibility of a delicate symbiosis between our two protagonists. In this story, the female will be no victim:

> It is a restless moment.
> She has kept her head lowered
> to give him a chance to come closer.
> But he could not for lack of courage.
> She turns and walks away.

When we first see Chow Mo-wan (Tony Leung Chiu-wai), a Cantonese native of Hong Kong who works as a journalist, and Su Li-zhen

(Maggie Cheung),[27] an immigrant from Shanghai who is a secretary in a shipping company, they are moving, coincidentally on the same day, into miniscule adjoining apartments in a crowded Hong Kong apartment building full of émigrés from Shanghai. It is 1962. Consistent with emotional relations in Wong's earlier films, their respective spouses aren't there; in fact, throughout the film—this is its justly celebrated technical tour de force—we hear the voices of their spouses, and sometimes even see them from behind, but we never see their faces.[28] Wong's use of offscreen space throughout this film is nothing short of brilliant.

Significantly, the movers inadvertently mix their belongings and slowly, very slowly (and, of course, much too slowly for a Hollywood film), they begin to interact and to get to know one another. Their first conversation, equally significantly, is about the absence of Li-zhen's husband and Mo-wan's wife, and thus those formidable absent presences are inserted front and center, yet invisibly, in the film. Ultimately Mo-wan and Li-zhen come to realize that their spouses seem always to be elsewhere at the same time. After comparing certain gifts each has received, they eventually conclude that the husband and wife are lovers. Through a series of role-playing "reenactments," Mo-wan and Li-zhen seek to understand how they could have been betrayed. While their mutual sorrow brings them closer together, however, they make a conscious if reluctant decision to "not be like them." To counter his increasing emotional involvement, Mo-wan eventually has himself transferred to Singapore, where Li-zhen visits his room but never contacts him. Coming to its emotional climax at the Angkor Wat temple in Cambodia in 1966, the film plays out, through a series of missed opportunities and bad decisions, as one of the most powerful renditions of mutually unrequited love in cinema history.

Like *Happy Together, In the Mood for Love* revels in its hopeless, languorous exploration of all the ways that love can be at once glorious and frustrating. In this film, the stance taken toward this universal truth is unabashedly romantic—perhaps Wong felt freer in a heterosexual context—whereas *Happy Together* tended to concentrate more on the frustration side of the equation. The romantic poets, after all, were able to find an ambivalent solace in the deliciousness of lovelorn suffering and melancholia, and it is that feeling that predominates in *In the Mood*.

Yet Wong's attention isn't really on the affair itself but rather on a theme that has obsessed him from the beginning. As he told Ciment and Niogret, "It seemed more interesting to look at the story through the prism of a past era, and the relation of the characters to their story years later. They keep their secret, and this secret to me seems the most interesting theme in the film" ("Entretien" [2000] 77). Time appears once again, in Wong's loving re-creation of the lovers' past and of his own, as well as being embodied in the grotesque clocks we see at regular intervals, especially in the office where Li-zhen works. Interestingly, however, there is virtually none of the obsessive date and time remembering of earlier films like *Days of Being Wild* and *Chungking Express*. Perhaps his characters are now too old for that kind of foolishness? Tony Rayns has poetically described the interweaving of these themes as "a gorgeously sensual *valse triste* that circles the themes of fidelity and sincerity in relationships before resolving itself into a requiem for a lost time and its values" ("In the Mood" 34).

Wong's emphasis on visual expressivity continues unabated, if in a somewhat different key. Everything is slowed, and the handheld camera is banished, but the film's form is hardly conventional. Objects and body parts are focused on in a new way and with a new intensity in shots with little narrative relevance, like the lingering shots of a woman's hand on the threshold of a door or the railing of a stairway—another homage to an important motif in the films of Michelangelo Antonioni, whom Wong has recognized as a major influence on this film.[29] Often, when the couple is walking together, the camera will somewhat perversely continue to remain on their midsection rather than, more conventionally, panning up to their faces as quickly as possible to preserve normal framing. Wong has said that this technique was employed, especially in interiors, to give an impression of what things looked like to a five-year-old—in other words, to him as a child—but he also seems to be playing with the viewer's expectations. For what is being stimulated here, beyond the spectator's own sexual desire, is his or her desire to see, always to see more, an impossible desire linked to the couple's impossible desire for each other.

More generally speaking, Wong has confessed that he was more attentive to the image in this film than in his previous films, since he had gotten lazy depending on Christopher Doyle to give him, automatically and wordlessly, exactly what he wanted. When Doyle had to be replaced by the celebrated Mark Li-ping, a frequent collaborator of the Taiwanese master Hou Hsiao-hsien and the Paris-based Vietnamese director Tran Anh-hung, Wong said, "I had to check things much more closely and to involve myself in the framing and lighting. It's a creative process in which I paid much more attention to the texture, and I think the visual aspect accords more closely with the content" (Ciment and Niogret, "Entretien" [2000] 79).

This visual aspect, for once, extends into costume as well as camera work and set design. A brilliant realization of opposing sexual forces is achieved in the more than twenty gorgeous dresses (*cheongsam*) that Li-zhen wears throughout the film. Form-fitting and tightly wound, even around her neck, they are thus at the same time highly sexual and highly repressed. The extremely vibrant floral motifs that sometimes decorate her *cheongsams* speak of a zestful life that can only be visually and thus symbolically represented and not actually lived. Most fascinatingly of all, Wong consistently uses a change of dress to signal the time gap between two juxtaposed scenes that we would otherwise think were the same scene. For example, the couple might be talking on the street, and then there's a cut to them from a different angle, in the same place, which seems temporally contiguous. Suddenly we notice—especially if we've already watched the film three times—that Li-zhen is wearing a different dress, and we realize that these are two different meetings. What is being underlined, of course, is the repetitiveness of their encounters.

Colors are used expressively, especially in the hotel room in which Mo-wan writes his martial-arts stories and in which they meet, apparently, to not have sex.[30] The colors are sickly and garish, and Li-zhen's movement down the hall to Mo-wan's room is accompanied by a series of jump cuts that occur nowhere else in the film. (These jump cuts provide a subtle index to the psychological difficulty she is experiencing by coming to his room.) We see him in a tight close-up, swathed in a sickly green color, and hear Li-zhen's knock. "I didn't think you'd come," he says. But then he adds quickly, "We won't be like them." When she leaves, her red coat rhymes with the heavy red curtains that cover the windows of the corridor; both here and later, when Mo-wan moves down this same hallway, we are reminded of the famous hotel hallway shot in Antonioni's *L'Avventura*. Here, though, the camera tracks backward, as Li-zhen, who continues walking forward, simultaneously distances herself from the camera, increasing the feeling of depth. As Wong's set designer, William Chang, put it, "'The colors I am using are very vivid, to contrast with the characters' restrained emotions'" (qtd. in Camhi 11), and in this scene the colors are the most vivid and disturbing of all, presumably to indicate the characters' inner turmoil. Again, as we have seen throughout this survey of Wong's films, the effect achieved is due as much to the colors and shapes as to the characters and the narrative line. As L. Codelli puts it, "it all coalesces thanks to a glowing and fragmented abstract impressionism. Orange and purple stains, against the blackest backgrounds, while violin solos vibrate" (102).

Most importantly, in virtually every shot in the film the camera moves, though always in a stately, lyrical manner. On one level, this movement adds to the film's rhythmic expressivity, but it also suggests that no single, fixed perspective is ever likely to bring us the truth about this couple (nor, by extension, about anything else). To further emphasize this point, in its trajectory in each shot or sequence, the camera almost always ends up shooting through some kind of hindrance, be it a doorway, a curtain, venetian blinds, a diaphanous lampshade, or one of the many mirrors that are found throughout the film. Wong has said that the point of this technique was to include the spectator in the scene, as though he or she were also a resident of this crowded location (Ciment and Niogret, "Entretien" [2000] 80). William Chang said that its purpose was to eliminate "'direct contact with the characters. We're looking at things from afar. It gives you space to think and feel rather than just identifying with the actors'" (qtd. in Camhi 11). But a more poetic explanation for this technique—and for the film's entire narrative strategy—comes at the end. The last intertitle reads as follows:

> He remembers those vanished years.
> As though looking through a dusty window pane,
>   the past is something he could see but not touch.
> And everything he sees is blurred and indistinct.

The implication is that whatever we see, and not only the past, is always elsewhere and always seen "through a dusty window pane."

The additional implication of this intertitle, especially coming where it does, is that everything we have thus far witnessed has been from the perspective of the male character. It might even be said that the voice-over of the central male protagonist, absent here for the first time since *As Tears Go By,* has been replaced by the *whole film* as a representation of Mo-wan's thoughts and feelings. In this vein, Paul Arthur has suggested that "although never explicitly bracketed as someone's remembered images, the story emanates as if from the coils of a dream or a trance-state. . . . That Wong evokes an *interiorized* landscape of desire as memory should be obvious. The narrow passages and cloistered chambers in which most of the action takes place are subtle, if by now rather familiar, tropes for the labyrinthine quality of the mind, its ceaseless movement along the same unending pathways of remembered experience" (40, 41).

As always for Wong, the editing is all. He told Ciment and Niogret that he shot more than thirty times the footage that he ended up using, a hugely expensive shooting ratio that is virtually unheard of in the contemporary film industry. "We edit scene by scene after shooting. It's the way we work. At the end, all I have to do is structure it. The process is not building up, but taking out things we don't want, and keeping what is essential and precise. That's why I shoot in chronological order" ("Entretien" [2000] 80).

But the editing in this film also has a strange binary logic to it. When people converse, we get the usual number of reverse shots, yet since there are almost no over-the-shoulder shots—the kind that conventionally mark conversations—the effect is jarring. The highly marked absent presence of the respective spouses also works thematically here. The intimacy they do share with Li-zhen and Mo-wan in some scenes seems strangely truncated and unnatural because, in a sense, they aren't there, and because the shot never reverses on *them.* Even the way they are (not) shown is expressive, as, for example, when we see the back of Mo-wan's wife's sensuous body entering a room, or the back of her head in the hotel mirror where she works as a receptionist, or when we glimpse the postcards for sale in her hotel, emblems of the farawayness these absent, illicit lovers represent in several different ways. (They are often away together, for example, in Japan.) It seems appropriate that the principal characters often speak to their spouses over the phone, since these are additional moments in which the spouses are absent and present at the same time. Another aspect of the editing, the brief fades

to black between scenes, adds to the solemnity of the film, while an occasional *refusal* to cut, with the camera lingering on an empty space after
a character has departed, heightens the sense of place, as though Wong
is reminding us more than ever that context must never be forgotten.
Similarly, we occasionally hear entire conversations between two people
while the camera remains resolutely focused on an empty hallway, say,
perhaps once again to underline the viewer's continual desire to see
more than he or she will ever be shown.

The moments of greatest expressive intensity come when the visual
track is reinforced by music. Wong has said that he played the music
for the cast and crew so that they would know, for example, how fast
a tracking shot should move (*In the Mood for Love* bonus DVD disc).
The conjunction of the powerful original score by Michael Galasso
(especially in evidence at the end of the film, which takes place at the
Angkor Wat Temple in Cambodia), the several Latin-themed romantic
songs sung by Nat King Cole, and the gorgeous composition by Shigeru
Umebayashi (which had already appeared in a Japanese film called
Yumeji, directed by Seijun Suzuki, ten years earlier) accompanies the
slowed-down, stretch-printed visuals that record the simplest of chores,
like going out for noodles.[31] The emotional effect of these scenes is
often heightened by a total absence of ambient sound. For this viewer
at least, despite (or because of) their conscious repetitiveness, these
deeply moving, aesthetically sublime moments express an essential
loneliness that perhaps afflicts all humans, not only our protagonists. Li-
zhen walks up the steps from the noodle shop, toward the street lamp,
and then the camera pans to Mo-wan going in the opposite direction,
visually linking them and rhyming their devastating isolation. At times,
this doleful, delicious waltz occurs in the rain, as in many other Wong
films, with the expected enhancement of the visual affect. Typically, the
repetition is purposeful, as Wong has said that he deliberately repeated
these scenes and the background music—as well as all those shots of
staircases and corridors—because "we can see these two people change
against this unchanging background. The repetitions help us to see the
changes" (Rayns, "In the Mood" 17). According to the director, the great
challenge was that, more than in any of his previous films, the actors
had to express themselves through their bodies, gestures, and glances
rather than through the dialogue (Ciment and Niogret, "Entretien"

[2000] 79), and it is in these scenes that this expression reaches its heartbreaking zenith.

Once the potential lovers begin to meet in the restaurant, their encounters, still centered on food (eating, again, is strongly correlated with emotion and the potential for human warmth),[32] take on an involved visual positioning that continues to reflect the psychological complexity of their nascent relationship. After an establishing shot of them facing each other in profile in the booth, from the side, we move to single shots of their heads (again, no over-the-shoulder shots), reminiscent of the straight-on framings in the films of the Japanese master Yasujiro Ozu that we've seen in Wong's earlier work,[33] as they come to understand, through the doubling of objects like ties and purses, that their partners are cheating on them with each other. There are playful zip pans from one figure to another and a strange pan that starts *behind* Mo-wan before it frames him. In a later scene in the same place, a two-shot seems to reverse their positions in the booth, but careful observation reveals that the original establishing shot, counterintuitively, was mounted from the other side of the booth, hence we're disoriented. (A common state of affairs in a film in which the viewer only realizes that it's another day because Li-zhen is wearing a different *cheongsam.*)

This playful disorientation is also related to an extremely significant, failed doubling that further suggests their disrupted psychological state, but which also manifests a fascinating thematic complexity (and thoroughly confuses first-time viewers). Seeking to understand how their spouses could have betrayed them, Li-zhen and Mo-wan, without preamble or explanation, engage in a series of role-playing scenes. The first occurs in the street. Mo-wan asks Li-zhen, "Should we stay out tonight?" Li-zhen replies, "My husband would never say that." Then roles are reversed, with Li-zhen taking the lead, saying the line of dialogue while playing lightly with Mo-wan's hands. The representation collapses, however, when Li-zhen, suddenly emotional, is unable to continue. In the restaurant, Li-zhen says that she doesn't know what to order "because I have no idea what your wife likes," which takes us aback at first, and then Mo-wan says virtually the same thing about her husband. We cut to an extreme close-up of some hot sauce on Li-zhen's plate (which, we learn, Mo-wan's wife enjoys), as Wong uses a zip pan between their two plates to stand in for the sexual encounter they both, at some level, obviously desire. As the French critic Philippe Rouyer has pointed out, what's interesting here is that "a love story (that of [Li-zhen] and [Mo-wan]) is born from the fictive representation of another romance and that, by a troubling irony, the two protagonists are led to mimic a break-up even before consummating their relationship" (74).

The best example of this play of substitution (and perhaps Wong's most mischievous moment in the film) comes when, in a much later scene, we see Li-zhen on the left, in a room, eating with chopsticks. Most viewers will have forgotten about the playacting by this point, and when we see the back of a man's head, on the right, we assume it's Mo-wan. Then, when she very seriously asks, "Do you have a mistress?" we think, wait, it's her husband. But this realization, in turn, is followed by a shock cut to Mo-wan: It's him after all, and they are just practicing for a future confrontation with her husband. Then they do it again, though she breaks down once more ("I didn't expect it to hurt so much") and can't continue. Throughout the film we are continually destabilized in this fashion, as when Mo-wan says something loving to Li-zhen, and, since we quickly become fully invested in their achieving happiness, we hope for the best. Then she replies, approvingly, "That sounded just like my husband. He's a real sweet-talker." As William Chang has pointed out, "'[E]verything that Maggie and Tony say to each other can also mean its opposite. Are they rehearsing their love, or is it real? It's quite complex'" (qtd. in Camhi 11). This questioning of the nature of representation, through a doubling that is repeatedly hidden and then revealed, provides a Brechtian complexity and intellectual depth that greatly exceeds what Wong has achieved in any of his earlier films. At the risk of overtheorizing a delicate film that achieves much of its effects through subtle indirection, I think this doubling also sheds new light on the nature of subjectivity. Just who *are* we, after all, and do we ever have the possibility of saying things to each other that aren't already lines of dialogue, scripted by our culture or society? Tony Rayns insists that Wong is always expressing "primary emotions" rather than, in a more postmodern fashion, mere signs or "cultural gestures" ("Charisma" 36). But since virtually all of the emotions in this film are prerehearsed or "quoted," as it were (including their own feelings for each other), is it really possible to make this distinction? It's this very impossibility that, at least in part, *In the Mood for Love* is concerned with.

The next time we experience the powerful combination of slowed-down visuals, absent ambient sound, and dramatically romantic strings comes when Li-zhen finds herself once again in a living room in the midst of the constricting social group she is a part of, while remaining at the same time completely removed from it. She and the camera meet, and she moves to the window, pensive. The flowers on her dress echo those on the curtains and the furniture (though in other scenes, their vitality clashes with more somber visual surroundings). The sound bridge, as before, takes us elsewhere, this time to Mo-wan's newspaper office. He too comes to a window and, in a lovely rhyming gesture, looks out. They are together and yet apart, in the same dynamic of absence and presence that structures the entire film.

This sequence is indicative of the film's overall structure: An extended series of short vignettes that have a cumulative effect aimed more at enhancing our emotional relation to the principal characters than our involvement with the plot, while keeping us distanced from them through other formal techniques at the same time. And so very often, as in this sequence, nothing, absolutely nothing, "happens." Mo-wan, here and elsewhere in the film, sits and smokes in a dark office with a light shining on him. The camera lingers over the beautiful patterns the smoke makes, and, amazingly, it works. It works precisely because of the evocative music that accompanies the narratively "empty" visuals and unleashes their expressivity. Here and in other sequences, this juxtaposition is accompanied by a slight slowing of the natural speed of the action, enough to partially transmogrify it into abstract visual expression. The music also serves as a sound bridge to link the two characters thematically and psychologically, as for example when we cut from Mo-wan smoking forlornly in his office to Li-zhen, alone in her office, spotted through the filtering, distorting curtains, as she always is.

But though external action remains minimal, it is at this point that the film's emotional trajectory begins to pick up speed. We next see them in the rain, speaking about the weather. An extreme long shot on the bare wall in the foreground recalls many decentered shots from *Happy Together*. Social convention forces them to wait before returning home, since even the banal fact that she might be seen with his umbrella may fatally compromise them. (The best example of the powerfully inhibiting effect of their social context comes earlier in the film, when Mo-wan's landlord returns unexpectedly from a social engagement and Li-zhen is trapped in Mo-Wan's room, though as always they are doing nothing forbidden. But appearances being all, Li-zhen must remain there for hours, while the neighbors play Mah-jongg all night, before she can escape the next day.) One of the paradoxical effects of this constantly present constricting social field is to place more cinematic emphasis on them as a couple, in opposition to the social field, as it were, thus relating them closely to the unhappy couple of *Happy Together*.

Despite the choking constraint of social obligation, their feelings for one another—and their desire—haven't been completely smothered. "I thought we wouldn't be like them," he says forlornly. "But I was wrong. You won't leave your husband. So I'd rather go away." She: "I didn't think you'd fall in love with me." He: "I didn't either. I was only curious to know how it started, and now I know. Feelings can creep up just like that." Their spouses may have finally abandoned the visual and aural field, but it is clear that they have never really disappeared.

The goodbye scene of the would-be lovers is over-the-top romantic. Nevertheless, or maybe because of that, it, too, works. In the slightest of slow-motion,[34] Mo-wan lets go of Li-zhen's hand (her wedding ring, ironically, in full view), and the camera stays on her face in extreme close-up as he remains far away in the background, out of focus. Then we discover, once again, that they are only *rehearsing* a separation that has not yet taken place and that, in fact, we never see. They playact through their emotional crisis, as if trying to manage it theatrically, and thus never reach their innermost selves, if such a place can be said to exist. They live within quotation marks and prewritten lines of dialogue. They put on an act because reality itself is too hard to bear. She sobs, and the strings reach a crescendo.

Transported by another sound bridge, we next see the backs of their heads in a cab; like Po-wing in *Happy Together*, she lets her head fall to her lover's shoulder. An extreme close-up on their hands follows, this time with his wedding ring on top. Subsequent meetings in the garish hotel room, or nonmeetings as they pine for each other on either side of the apartment wall that separates them, result only in further frustration.

We cut to an extreme long shot of a blue sky and a palm tree. A title informs us that it is now 1963 and we are in Singapore, where Mo-wan has asked to be transferred in order to escape his heartbreak.

He searches his hotel room, finds a lipsticked cigarette, and knows that Li-zhen has been there. Of course, they do not meet. Mo-wan tells his friend and alter ego, the sensualist Ping (played by Siu Ping-lam, Wong's prop man), a poetic story about putting a secret in a hole in a tree, closing it up, and leaving it there forever. Ping's earthy response: "I'd just go get laid." What follows is a curious, out-of-sequence flashback on Li-zhen's visit to his hotel room in Singapore, but from the consciousness of the film, as it were, not from that of any particular character. We witness her putting the cigarette in her mouth, and placing it in the ashtray, as a kind of signal. Seen through a barely functional mirror—again, the motif of the impossibility of whole vision and complete understanding—she telephones him but is unable to speak when he answers.

We cut back to Hong Kong. It is now 1966, three years later. Li-zhen, visiting her old landlady Mrs. Suen, has a different hairstyle and is worried about the "situation" in Hong Kong, the first overt reference in the film to a political theme, though it has been there indirectly all along (1966 is the period of the pro-mainland riots in Hong Kong, inspired by the Cultural Revolution). Mrs. Suen, who has been the primary representative of the constricting social world throughout the film, is planning, like Auntie in *Days of Being Wild* (and she is played by the same actress, Rebecca Pan), on emigrating to the United States. Wong has said that he focused on this date because the film is "about the end of a period. The year 1966 marks a turning point in Hong Kong's history. The Cultural Revolution in the mainland had lots of knock-on effects, and forced Hong Kong people to think hard about their future. . . . So 1966 is the end of something and the beginning of something else" (Rayns, "In the Mood" 15).

Li-zhen buys the apartment from Mrs. Suen. Then Mo-wan visits the apartment next door, where he lived, but the original owner is gone. Naturally, the once would-be lovers miss each other again. A poetic intertitle, meaning different things on both the personal and political levels, tells us, "That era has passed. Nothing that belonged to it exists any more." We hear shoes skittering across the floor and discover that Li-zhen now has a son, signaling a kind of closure and, on one level, a final denial of the hope that their love might ever be consummated. But Wong tantalizingly leaves open the question as to who the father of the child might be.[35]

Finally, we arrive in Cambodia, apparently immediately after. We watch a newsreel of the meeting between the French president Charles de Gaulle and Prince Norodom Sihanouk, and this offers an apparent political context, but only indistinctly.[36] We then discover that we are in Angkor Wat, the site of the legendary Cambodian temples, and Mo-wan is whispering his secret into a hole in one of the ancient buildings, as the camera circles around him in a grandiloquent gesture reminiscent of the closing shots of the waterfalls and the lighthouse in *Happy Together.* A monk's head, backlit and out of focus, occupies the bulk of the frame, with Mo-wan a mere speck in the lower right corner. It is a powerful moment. The long ancient corridors, like the old streets seen earlier, contrast silently but intensely with the specificity and nowness of his secret, his pain. We realize suddenly that what he is going through, and has gone through, must be seen *sub specie aeternitatis.* There is always a larger world—here represented, in current political terms, by the specificity of the newsreel of de Gaulle's visit and in longer historical terms by the ancientness of the temple—that dwarfs the problems of any given person. Individuals have always suffered, and they always will, and this is a secret that all of us know and could, ourselves, tell the hole in the wall. As Wong has put it in the U.S. press kit, "At first, I thought *In the Mood for Love* to be like chamber music. All the things happen in a certain space: in apartments, in restaurants, on street corners. It's something very intimate, in an enclosed environment—people are trying to cover it. At the end of the film, I thought we should provide another perspective, and I wrote something which is totally different: something with histories and a more spiritual side" (17–18).

The music stops, and the camera continues tracking, suggesting that life always goes on, beyond any individual life. Birds continue to chirp; like history, nature will always outlive us as well. Wong seems, finally, to have begun to understand the pain and impossibility of adult love in the larger context of ubiquitous, implacable human pain. Remarkably, it's something rather greater and more profound than—yet still amazingly similar to—the teenage heartbreak lingered over in his earlier movies. It's the same thing, finally, but it's also different.

The final title tells all we need to know and retrospectively explains the film's technique:

He remembers those vanished years.
As though looking through a dusty window pane,
    the past is something he could see but not touch.
And everything he sees is blurred and indistinct.

The longing, the frustration, the desire that will never be satisfied: still there after seven films and all this time. But now it's all part of something bigger than any one of us. The story's context has transcended the merely social to become the universal. As Wong has put it with elegant simplicity, "I think *In the Mood for Love* is the most difficult film in my career so far, and also one of the most important. I'm very proud of it" (*In the Mood for Love* press kit, 18).

2046

After *In the Mood for Love*, Wong made a delightful short, set in a present-day convenience store, called *In the Mood for Love 2001*. Starring Maggie Cheung and Tony Leung once again, the film was shown at the Cannes Film Festival in 2001. He has also made a fascinating segment called "The Follow" in a series of commercials that well-known directors have shot for BMW, known collectively as "The Hire" and available at <bmwfilms.com>. Employing all of his trademark techniques, the short has had wide exposure on the Internet. Wong has also continued to make music videos with Faye Wong and Tony Leung, and there has been talk since 2001 of his having made one segment of a three-part film called *Eros* with Michelangelo Antonioni and Steven Soderbergh, but nothing has been seen of this long-promised film as of this writing.

After this book was already in press, Wong's latest film, *2046*, was shown in the competition at the Cannes International Film Festival in May 2004, where I was able to see it, alas, only a single time. Typically, Wong managed to "finish" the film at literally the last minute, causing the press screening to be postponed from its scheduled morning slot to 7:30 in the evening—a virtually unique occurrence in the history of the festival—owing to the fact that the subtitling, music, and so on had not yet been fully coordinated. Based on the print shown, I would say that the film remains to some extent unfinished, especially since Wong playfully contended during the press conference following the screening that

Figure 16. *In the Mood for Love*: Once again, lovers (Tony Leung Chiu-wai and Maggie Cheung) in a taxi.

it was "complete for now."[37] Consider the following addendum, then, as a kind of interim, informal scouting report. (The film is as intricate and convoluted as any of his previous films, so the reader should bear in mind that the plot summary and brief explication that follow are provisional and probably mistaken in some particulars.)

2046 is set in the 1960s, and Tony Leung Chiu-wai appears once again as the former journalist Chow Mo-wan, the character he played in Wong's previous film, *In the Mood for Love*. The locale at the beginning is identified as "Singapore, 1966," but we don't see Mo-wan until he has returned from Singapore, where he had gone near the end of the previous film after losing the love of his life, Li-zhen (Maggie Cheung). Perhaps because he has been disappointed in love, the ultrasensitive Mo-wan has become a completely different man, taking his sexual pleasure when and where he can and refusing to allow any woman to tie him down. The contrast between the two versions of Mo-wan is actually quite startling and will be difficult for most viewers who know the earlier film to negotiate, at least at first. At the Cannes press conference, Tony Leung said, "This film is about a man who is trying to get rid of his past. Wong told me that it was the same character as before, but that I should treat him as a completely new character. This was quite different and challenging to do, so I asked Wong if I could at least have a moustache to represent this change in the same character for me." Leung was granted the moustache and, indeed, it does help make the transition for the viewer as well.

Mo-wan is a writer of science fiction, having graduated from pornography, and on May 22, 1967, as he informs us, he has begun a novel called *2046*. Politically, this date is significant as the year prior to the end of the fifty-year interim period that the mainland Chinese government has promised to Hong Kong, the former British colony, before its complete political and legal absorption into the People's Republic. Virtually no mention of this political situation, however, occurs in the film, and Mo-wan claims that the date he uses for his novel came from the room number of the hotel he once stayed in, which viewers may recognize from *In the Mood for Love*. Mo-wan does refer liberally, and interestingly, to various demonstrations and riots that took place in Hong Kong during the 1960s as specific chronological markers, but this is as political as things ever get. Wong stated clearly during the Cannes press conference, "I was inspired by the situation in Hong Kong, but it has never been my intention to make films with any political content whatsoever. I'm more interested in the film [itself]. This film is about promises." Yet while Wong emphasized the many mistakes made by Mo-wan, and, more generally, the many chances all of us miss in life, he also said, "How do you deal with your past? This can also be a question for a city. This is the question of the film."

Interspersed sparingly throughout the film are dystopian scenes, generated by Mo-wan's ink pen rushing across his pages, that paint a bleak future of alienating cyborgs and apparent dysfunction. Interestingly, though, 2046 is continuously presented not so much as a date but rather as a *place* that people seek to arrive at by means of an ultrafast bullet train, in order to preserve or relocate their memories. As Mo-wan (or his fictional narrator) tells us in voiceover, though, we can't know any of this for sure, since he is the only person who has ever returned from 2046.

In the meantime, back in the 1960s, where, despite its title, nearly all the film takes place, Mo-wan is living, as he was in *In the Mood for Love*, in exceedingly tight quarters. This time he is frequenting what is apparently a hotel owned by Mr. Wang (Wang Sum), who has two daughters. One is very young and "precociously" interested in Mo-wan. The other is Wang Jing Wen, played by Faye Wong, the pop singer whom we last saw as the irrepressible gamine Faye in the second part of *Chungking Express*. Jing Wen has a Japanese boyfriend, a situation her father is not too happy about, and we see her practicing Japanese phrases throughout the film. (The brief scenes actually set in 2046 feature the Japanese pop star Takuya Kimura and employ Japanese dialogue because, according to Wong, Mo-wan's novel is based on the relations between Jing Wen and her Japanese boyfriend.) Mo-wan befriends Jing Wen and agrees to receive the letters from her boyfriend for her; later in the film he becomes romantically interested in her himself. Typically for a Wong film, though, she is thinking of someone else. In voiceover, Mo-wan sadly bemoans the harshness of timing, that perennial Wong theme, since he would have had a completely different life had he met her first.

At another point, Mo-wan is down on his luck in Singapore and takes to gambling, which only makes matters worse. He is befriended by a mysterious lady who gambles, and wins, for him. She always wears a single black glove, and she ultimately tells him that her name is Su Li-zhen, which is the maiden name of the married woman in *In the Mood for Love* and, of course, the name of the woman in *Days of Being Wild,* both played by Maggie Cheung. (Mo-wan expressly mentions, in voiceover, that years ago a married woman he was in love with had the same name.) To make matters even more complicated, Su Li-zhen is played by the iconic Chinese actress Gong Li, while Maggie Cheung makes a special, tiny appearance as a cyborg on the train that goes to 2046 (though some who saw the film claimed she wasn't really in it at all).

The central emotional focus of the film, however, is on another woman, Bai Ling, a prostitute who lives in the same hotel as Mo-wan. Ling is played by the most popular actress in Chinese cinema today, Zhang Ziyi, who starred in *Crouching Tiger, Hidden Dragon.* Ling and Mo-wan have a playful relationship that includes several passionate lovemaking sessions, but, gradually, and tragically for her, Ling begins to fall in love with him. Mo-wan, however, perhaps terminally wounded emotionally by his failed encounter with Li-zhen in the previous film, refuses to commit. Near the end, there are several powerful scenes in which Ling weeps inconsolably over the impossibility of the fulfillment of her love for Mo-wan.

As can be seen by this meager outline, many of Wong's perennial themes remain present in this new film: the painful contradictions of love; the persistence of longing, memory, and regret; and the hopelessness of ever recapturing, modifying, or getting rid of the past. Wong's trademark obsession with the onward rush of time appears again as well—but interestingly, only once does an actual clock appear in this film (though exact dates abound)—and the director even pokes fun at himself with an intertitle in-joke that says "10 Hours Later," then "100 Hours Later," then "1,000 Hours Later." A new wrinkle is added to the familiar theme, however, with the motif of borrowing or buying time, as one would do with a prostitute. There is much made of Mo-wan paying Ling for her sexual services, in other words, her time, and Ling at first refuses a gift because this would change the nature of their relationship. Then later, in a teasing reversal, Mo-wan talks about being paid by her. They joke about whether there is anything that Mo-wan, an otherwise carefree soul, would not lend someone. Near the climax of the film he admits that there is one thing that he wouldn't lend, strongly implying that he means his commitment, and thus his time.

Offering his own typically cryptic explanation of the film's themes, Wong said in the director's statement that accompanies the press kit that "there is a need in all of us to have a place to hide or store certain memories, thoughts, impulses, hopes, and dreams. These are part of our lives that we can't resolve or best not act upon but at the same time we are afraid to jettison them. For some, this is a physical place; for others, it is a mental space, and for a few it is neither." Speaking more informally, he said at the press conference that *2046*

was originally meant as a continuation of *In the Mood for Love*. I was like the writer. *In the Mood* and *2046* were started at the same time, but I decided I didn't want to do a sequel, I wanted to do something different. I wanted Tony to be completely different this time, but the more I wanted to make him different, the more I kept coming back to *In the Mood*. I was trying to portray someone trying to get away, but the more you try to get away, the closer you come. But if you just let it go, one day the past memories may leave you, and this is the message of the film.

Virtually half of the scenes in 2046 occur in conjunction with eating of some sort, a motif we have seen over and over in Wong's work, and the continual gesture of characters *looking* at one another is even more highly developed than it was in *Mood*. Perhaps most entertainingly, 2046 contains a host of intriguing references to several of Wong's earlier films, mostly in terms of situations and characters, much as he had undertaken in *Fallen Angels*, another self-conscious summary of his oeuvre. For one thing, both the "tropical" theme music of *Days of Being Wild* as well as the character of Lulu/Mimi (played once again by Carina Lau) reappear. There is the joyous sexual horsing around that recalls similar moments between Yuddy and Lulu/Mimi in the same film. Many times we see Mo-wan leaning over into a mirror to comb his slicked-down hair, just like Tony Leung's character, Smirk, did at the end of *Days of Being Wild*. There is also a reference to the "bird who couldn't land" motif from *Days*, as well as to the telling of secrets to a hole, then covering it up, which powerfully concluded *In the Mood for Love*. The sensualist Ah Ping (Ping Lam Siu), Mo-wan's sidekick and alter ego, also shows up once again. As with Li-zhen in *Mood*, we often find out we're in a different day solely by virtue of the fact that Ling is wearing a different *cheongsam*. And all the sex that we didn't get in *Mood*, but perhaps at some level wanted, is here in spades, in what was obviously meant by Wong as a deliberate contrast. (In fact, there's one specific scene that looks exactly like a scene from *Mood* except that it ends with the enormously passionate kiss on those red, red lips that some viewers may have ardently desired in the earlier film and didn't get.)

Wong's familiar crew is on hand once again—Christopher Doyle as director of photography (this time abetted by Kwan Pung Leung and Lai Yiu Fai), William Chang as production designer and editor, and Shigeru Umebayashi as composer—hence it is no surprise that the film is, formally speaking, quite similar to *Mood*. It is marked by the same angularities and off-center framing, the same refractions and divisions that result from countless mirroring images, and many shots are of anonymous feet, or of a skirt-clad torso moving by in slow motion without the character being identified. There are familiar moments of sublime beauty where cigarette smoke wafts upward in slight slow-motion, or a character holds a hand up to a mirror in a subtle, desperate gesture. One repeated shot of the outside of the hotel features the bright neon we've seen since *As Tears Go By*, and there is also the shot of quickly moving people around a solitary figure that we saw in *Chungking Express*, but now the people move more slowly. Once again, there is the climactic taxi ride we've seen in *Happy Together* and *In the Mood for Love*, with the couple in the back seat, though this time it is the man with his head on the shoulder of the woman. (By contrast, the futuristic scenes are purposely dark and uninviting, and, for the most part, unnaturally speeded up—2046 does not look like a very inviting place to be.) As always, music plays a crucial role, whether it be epic-sounding (though with a hint of the electronic and slightly distorted), as at the beginning of the film, the Spanish romantic music sprinkled throughout, or the Nat King Cole rendition of "Chestnuts Roasting on an Open Fire" that appears motivically throughout the film when Mo-wan meets Ling on Christmas Eve, several years in a row. Even more complicated—too complicated for this hasty summary—is the function of the opera arias that appear throughout, which Wong has said in earlier interviews were meant to provide a three-part structure for the film, each part based upon a nineteenth-century opera (*Madame Butterfly, Carmen,* and *Tannhäuser*). As Wong told Leslie Camhi, "'opera is about promises, betrayals and myths'" (26) and thus provides a perfect setting to explore his familiar themes.

I hope that this modest addendum indicates how much there will be to discuss when this complex, exciting new film opens commercially in 2005.

Notes

1. Art films, as David Bordwell has famously pointed out, are themselves part of a genre with readily identifiable characteristics ("Art Cinema"). I think it remains useful to distinguish the art film from "genre films" that can be defined more conventionally, such as the gangster film.

2. The VHS version has several cutaways to this shot, while the DVD version has only one. (Though I have not undertaken a frame-by-frame comparison of these two versions, both of which I have used in my analysis, my impression is that they differ in some formal details.)

3. Cheung has appeared in almost all of Wong's films, becoming, in Chuck

Stephens's felicitous phrase, his "decentered muse." According to Wong, the roles Maggie Cheung had been offered before *As Tears Go By* were quite weak, so she didn't take herself seriously as an actress. He also noticed that the more lines she had, the more nervous she got. "But if she had fewer lines," he told Bérénice Reynaud, "she started to relax and I noticed that she really knew how to *move*. So I cut most of her lines, to concentrate on her actions, on the most intimate movements of her body, and her acting became excellent" (Reynaud, "Entretien" 38).

4. Tony Rayns attributes Yuddy's "absurd" name to the film's first subtitler ("*Ah Fei*" 12). In the most recent version, on DVD, the name is improbably rendered "York" in the subtitles. Since all other critics, including Rayns, use the name Yuddy, I have as well.

5. Wong told one interviewer that he got the idea for the film's repetitive structure from Manuel Puig's novel *Heartbreak Tango* (Reynaud, "Entretien" 37).

6. Wong told Tony Rayns that his original idea was to start by focusing on the male characters, but "Part two [never filmed] would have centred on the Maggie Cheung and Carina Lau characters, showing how they try to overcome the traumas caused by their failed love affairs" ("Poet" 14).

7. The motif shows up fleetingly elsewhere, as when Yuddy's stepmother makes a disparaging comment about flying. And, according to Curtis K. Tsui at least, the "Fei" in the film's Cantonese title, in addition to referring to wild youth, means "fly" and thus also recalls the bird motif (101).

8. A propos of this image, Wong has said, "I sometimes use an image without any actors in it at all, like the phone booth in *Days of Being Wild*. You can show change by showing things that don't change" (Rayns, "Poet" 14).

9. Although *Ashes of Time* actually opened two months after *Chungking Express*, it was begun several years earlier, and thus I will follow standard practice and consider it before *Chungking Express*. See Teo (197) for more details.

10. Wong's memory is slightly off here. Martha signals her love for Ethan by the way she caresses his cloak in his absence, an action that is witnessed by Reverend Clayton.

11. See Brunette and Wills (chap. 4), for a discussion of the aesthetic and philosophical consequences of this gap.

12. A similar expressive gap occurs occasionally between the dialogue and the visuals. Curtis K. Tsui describes one moment when we hear a conversation, but the lips of the two participants in the conversation, whom we see in the frame, aren't moving (106).

13. The relation of the voiceover to the narrative is even more complex in this film, as when Ouyang Feng seems in his monologue to be referring directly to a visualized scene (a swordsman cutting Yin/Yang's outer garment while fighting in the lake, revealing her breasts) that he cannot have seen himself. At times, it seems as though he's watching the film along with us.

14. Wong playfully told Michel Ciment that he used numbers for this and the other male character in the film because he has trouble thinking of names. More seriously, he said the numbering gesture "gave a certain flavor." While reading nineteenth-century Russian novelists, he said, he got so confused with the names that he welcomed the simplicity of Kafka, who, according to Wong, named all his heroes "K" ("Entretien" 45).

15. Wong says the idea came to him because this is the kind of product that is sold in the convenience stores in which much of the film was shot in order to make use of available lighting during night scenes. "What I found ironic was that the cans that were supposed to preserve the freshness of a food product themselves had a expiration date. Even freshness can be spoiled" (Reynaud, "Entretien" 38).

16. His name, as rendered in the subtitled version of his voiceover, is He Qiwu, which is the same name as undercover policeman number 223 in *Chungking Express*, a "coincidence" that will be discussed below. Bordwell calls him Ho Chi Mo, but his police photo in one scene shows his name as Ho Chi Moo, which is what he will be called here.

17. The actress who plays this part is also called Charlie Young. I have been unable to determine whether this is the same Charlie Young who played the girl with the eggs in *Ashes of Time*, but they are vastly different in appearance.

18. However, she's played by a different actress.

19. The film's Chinese title, *Cheun gwong tsa sit*, has been variously translated as "Spring Light Leaking" (Stokes and Hoover), "Spring Brilliance Suddenly Pours Out" (Bordwell), and "unexpected revelation of scenes of spring" in Chow (who also, without explanation or justification, says that it's a "metaphor for the surprising display of erotic sights" ["Nostalgia" 230–31]).

20. The voice-over is also used occasionally to provide a fresh, if ironic, perspective on things. For example, after Yiu-fai has begun working in the kitchen of a Chinese restaurant, we suddenly hear voice-over from a character we don't even know, another Chinese kitchen helper named Chang with whom Yiu-fai becomes friends. The most immediate and welcome effect is that this voiceover temporarily relieves us of the claustrophobia of the couple's overheated relationship and gives us, suddenly, an *outside* and thus ironic perspective on everything (when Chang hears Yiu-fai talking to the estranged Po-wing on the phone, he mistakenly thinks out loud, "He must be in love").

21. This scene was highly overdetermined for the actors, it appears. Wong told *Positif* that he normally doesn't ask his actors to play characters that are totally unlike them and hence often borrows a lot from each actor's personality. "When they began to feel more comfortable after a couple of days, I let them improvise more, especially in the bed scenes. In fact, I presented the situation to them and then they improvised while the camera rolled." Wong said that Po-wing's character is actually very close to Leslie Cheung's, so the actor felt comfortable with his part. Unfortunately, this was not the case for Tony Leung.

Wong's goal, he said, was to destabilize Leung, since he always seems so subtle and concentrated. "The first day he did the sex scene, and he insisted on keeping his underpants on. He was so upset that he didn't say anything for the next three days." Leslie Cheung, however, dared the heterosexual director: "You want to tell a love story between two men. I want to see just how far you're going to go" (Ciment and Niogret, "Entretien" [1997] 13).

22. As usual, Wong started filming with only the sketchiest of treatments, and he continued to write dialogue right up to the last minute before shooting each scene. The story told in the final film was constructed after the fact in the editing room. Doyle writes in his diary of having to shoot different endings to allow Wong various options. For example, it wasn't known at the moment of shooting whether Yiu-fai's visit to the falls would end up being real or an imaginary flash-forward dream sequence, so they shot it both ways. Doyle also says that when new actors like Shirley Kwan and Chen Chang arrived, "they idle[d] in their rooms waiting for their roles to materialize, while Wong [hid] in nearby coffee shops hoping for the same. . . . Now that they're here, we fret over what to do with them, and over the thematic justifications for them even to be here" (Doyle 17). The scenes including Shirley Kwan were not used in the final version of the film. In a tantalizing prefatory note to Doyle's diary, Tony Rayns speaks of "countless scenes and incidents devised by Wong during the shoot" that were never used in the film, "including an extended episode in which the Leslie Cheung character became a cross-dressing hooker" (Doyle 14).

23. For an alternative view of these emotional dynamics, see Rey Chow, "Nostalgia." Chow invokes Lacan and Derrida yet still manages to produce a thoroughly pedestrian reading of the film. The best source for subtle insights, however, may not be an author who describes Po-wing (she idiosyncratically and without explanation spells his name Bo-Wing, unlike virtually every other critic writing on the film, and unlike what it says on his passport) as an "irresponsible scumbag" (233) and "a jerk who fucks around" (236).

24. The Mandarin title of the film is *Hua Yang Nian Huo,* while the Cantonese title is *Faa Yeung Niu Wao.* Both mean something like "Flowerlike Years" or "The Age of Flowers," which can refer to a woman's beauty in her prime, according to the director, but is also meant to refer to the 1960s, the period in the history of Hong Kong portrayed in the film (DVD bonus disc). It is also the name of the pop song by Zhou Xuan, recorded in the 1930s or 1940s, which we hear on the radio near the end of the film. Further complicating the reference, Wong and his editor/art director William Chang made a two-minute compilation film, with the same title, which is composed of clips from earlier Hong Kong movies. It is available on the DVD of *In the Mood for Love.*

25. This poet of antirealist, expressive cinema even went so far as to complain to Michel Ciment and Hubert Niogret that too many other filmmakers had gotten the *facts* wrong when trying to re-create the lives of immigrants from Shanghai. "My intention is to show people what the Shanghai community really was like" ("Entretien" [2000] 79).

26. A sex scene was shot, but Wong told Tony Rayns that he cut it at the last moment. "I suddenly felt I didn't want to see them having sex. And when I told William Chang [Wong's production designer, editor, and closest collaborator], he said he felt the same but hadn't wanted to tell me!" ("In the Mood" 17). The barely visible (though quite audible) scene is available on the DVD. Its inclusion in the finished version would have clearly made it a completely different kind of film.

27. Significantly or not, this is the same name as Maggie Cheung's character in *Days of Being Wild*. She says during a "making-of" minidocumentary on the DVD of the film that, to keep her from posing incessant questions about her character, Wong told her that she could consider Su Li-zhen as the same woman ten years later. This strikes me as a highly implausible suggestion.

28. Wong claims that they were never shown "mostly because the central characters were going to enact what they thought their spouses were doing and saying. In other words, we were going to see both relationships—the adulterous affair and the repressed friendship—in the one couple. It's a technique I learned from Julio Cortazar, who always has this kind of structure. It's like a circle, the head and tail of a snake meeting" (Rayns, "In the Mood" 17).

29. Wong says that the scenes that take place in the street, in front of old walls, remind him of certain shots in Antonioni's film and were intended as an homage to the Italian master (Ciment and Niogret, "Entretien" [2000] 80).

30. We also get a glimpse of this room, in an apparent flash-forward, early in the film. The difficulty of understanding the meaning and logic of individual scenes cannot be overestimated. I have watched this film attentively at least five times, and even on the fifth time I was seeing narrative connections that had eluded me earlier.

31. The Latin music, according to Wong, was a temporal reference to the kind of music he heard on the radio throughout his childhood. Since most of the musicians in Hong Kong came from the Philippines, the Latin influence is easy to account for. Most importantly for the director, Nat King Cole was his mother's favorite singer (Ciment and Niogret, "Entretien" [2000] 79).

32. The film was originally to be a study of food in three parts, influenced by Anthelme Brillat-Savarin's classic text *The Physiology of Taste; or, Meditations on Transcendental Gastronomy*. The first part was to be a story about the relation between the owner of a fast-food joint and his customers, and the second about a kidnapper and the person he kidnaps. The third part, which is now the entirety of the film, was originally planned to be only thirty minutes long and was to focus solely on the noodle shop, the restaurant, and the stairs. Originally the story continued to 1972, but Wong, feeling that things were getting out of control, stopped the action in 1966 for reasons concerning the political theme (Ciment and Niogret, "Entretien" [2000] 77).

In the press kit that accompanied the U.S. release, however, Wong gave a somewhat different description of the original conception: "One story was called 'Tales from the Kitchen,' a love story between a chef and a cashier. The second story was called 'Handsome Devil in Campbell's Soup,' a love story between the owner of a supermarket and a customer. He wants to express his feelings, but he's too shy, so he keeps writing love letters to this woman by the alphabet in the Campbell's soup. He makes the soup every night and drinks it" (15).

Interestingly, Wong also told Ciment and Niogret that western audiences would be missing a lot of chronological clues embedded in the film's food. "Shanghai cooking is connected to the seasons in a very precise way. The food tells you if it's March, May, or June. Maggie [Li-zhen] is asked to stay for dinner to have won-ton, which is only eaten with certain vegetables that are available only in June and July. Thus we know precisely that it's June or July, 1962" (77).

33. A shot that is focused on Li-zhen's empty slippers, from a different scene, is also a clear homage to a famous shot in Ozu's masterpiece, *Tokyo Story* (1953).

34. Wong has said that "everything in this film is expressed by the bodies and how they move. There were some details that I wanted to show. The slow-motion doesn't express the action, but the environment. . . . It was there to capture a certain space, a certain ambiance" (Ciment and Niogret, "Entretien" [2000] 80).

35. Wong told Ciment and Niogret, "I wanted to keep that ambiguity. Maybe it's his child. The age is right, but that doesn't prove anything. We just don't know" ("Entretien" [2000] 78).

36. Wong has said that he included this newsreel because "DeGaulle is part of the colonial history that's about to fade away" [Rayns, "In the Mood" 16]. Elsewhere, however, the director has said that he "had to give Tony a reason to be there. We looked at all the newsreels, and the big event of the era was the visit by Charles De Gaulle to Cambodia. I love this document: it not only evokes this event, but it has a wake-up function as well. The whole story is like a dream, and then comes this true, factual element" (Ciment and Niogret, "Entretien" [2000] 78).

37. According to Wong, "The reason it was late was that I used CGI for some images at the beginning and at the end, and three different companies—from Hong Kong, China, and Paris—were involved, and the stuff didn't match." At the press conference, the director alternated between claiming that what we had seen was the final version of the film and suggesting that it "was the final version for May 2004. If I had three more weeks, the film would be different, and if I had three more months, it would be different still." But he also said that he knew he had to accept that it was finished, that he was thrilled, and that finally the standing joke—that the film's title represented its completion date—was now over.

Interview with Wong Kar-wai
(Toronto International Film Festival, 1995)

The following interview was conducted by the author at the Toronto International Film Festival in September 1995, following the screening of Wong Kar-wai's fifth film, *Fallen Angels*. It is published here for the first time. Since *Fallen Angels* was the first Wong film I had ever seen, the interview doesn't go very deeply into his work. Nevertheless, some of the information the director provided at the time still seems worthy of being more widely disseminated.

PETER BRUNETTE: I told a friend of mine today that "I have seen the future of cinema, and it's *Fallen Angels.*" I'm really quite serious about this.

WONG KAR-WAI: Why? Why do you say that?

PB: I thought it was the most imaginative handling of visuals and sound that I have seen in my life. But it's not only that. It's the irony, it's your use of the genre conventions. It has depth to it, and it plays with the idea of depth and surface. But I want you to talk about all this. I know what I think about it. First, tell me something about your background.

WKW: I was born in Shanghai, and I came to Hong Kong with my parents when I was five years old, in 1963. We spent a lot of time in cinemas. And my father always wanted me to learn all the literature, the classic Chinese literature. So I had big books when I was thirteen. My brother and sister—they are much older than me, and they stayed in Shanghai—always spoke in letters about things I didn't know at the time, like Balzac and Tolstoy and Gorky.

PB: All the Russian stuff.

WKW: Yes. So, because I wanted to communicate with them, I tried to read that kind of book. Big books. But I like Balzac. And after that, I got interested in Japanese literature, because it is easy to find Chinese translations. After that, all kinds of books. South American, American. Now I'm quite interested in Raymond Carver.

PB: Did you go to film school?

WKW: No, I went to movies instead. I was studying graphic design at the Polytechnic in Hong Kong for a while, after secondary school. Then the local TV station began offering a course for production designers and directors. In fact, most of the talent in the Hong Kong film industry came from TV. And you got paid 750 dollars a month. So I thought it was a good idea, since you could go to school and also make money. So I just joined the course, and then after a year I became a production trainee. And then the producer asked me to write scripts because I had a bunch of different ideas when we had the production meetings. Then I became a part-time scriptwriter.

PB: This was about what year?

WKW: I think it was 1979.

PB: So you wrote a script . . .

WKW: So I wrote a script for TV, and then after that, because the film industry at that time was quite prosperous, I became a freelance scriptwriter, and then I joined a big company, then a small company, then a gangster company, things like that. After six years as a scriptwriter, I became a director for my first film, *As Tears Go By.* My next film, *Days of Being Wild,* was much more complicated. In *Chungking Express* you have only two stories, but in *Days of Being Wild* you have six stories. And it was supposed to be a two-part film. One happened in 1960, and the other in 1966. But after the first one, because the film was so expensive and didn't do much business, because it wasn't a very conventional Hong Kong movie. . . . After that, I made a martial arts film, which is called *Ashes of Time*, and then *Chungking Express*, which has two stories. But to me it's not two stories, it's just day and night. But it is two stories with different actors and actresses. *Chungking Express* was supposed to have three stories. The first story was about the drug dealer, which I think at that time I was trying to do it like a Cassavetes story, like his film *Gloria*. I had that genre in my mind. So the woman has a blonde wig and a raincoat, which is very funny. In the second story, I'm trying to do it like a Jacques Demy kind of musical, *Lola*. Originally, we had a third story, which was about a killer. There I was thinking about Jean-Pierre Melville's film *Le Samourai* with Alain Delon.

PB: And this third story has instead become *Fallen Angels*?

WKW: Yes, because when I made the first one, the first part, I had so much fun, and it was already too long. So I just skipped the third part. It's a story about cops and gangsters. But no gangster/cop story, you know. It is a woman killer, a cop, and then a man killer. So I just changed the sexes. In fact, it's the same story to me. But after the first one, I thought it was already too long. So I just had the woman part, and the Jacques Demy part, and I skipped the third one. And then, after *Chungking Express* was finished, I realized the story still interested me. I tried to develop it into *Fallen Angels*, which would focus on the man killer. Then I took the story from *Chungking Express* about the girl who sneaks into other people's apartments, and in *Fallen Angels* I have a boy sneak into other people's shops. So it was quite a reversal.

PB: You don't seem very interested in narrative in *Fallen Angels*.

WKW: In fact, most of my films are quite loosely constructed, because I'm more interested in characters, people. And I'm quite interested in a South American writer, Manuel Puig. When I was a scriptwriter, we tried to make the story very simple, very straightforward, because in Hong Kong, you have to make the audience understand the film within five or ten minutes. But when I was making my second film, *Days of Being Wild*, I came across a book, [Puig's] *Heartbreak Tango*, and it was very interesting, because the structure was just chopped down and constructed with different orders. But it works at the end. So I'm trying to do this kind of thing.

PB: You seem to be interested in absurdism, too, in an interesting way. I mean, there's just so much going on in your films I don't even know what kind of questions to ask you. I mean it's . . . the wide-angle lens, the interiors, those long interiors, those horrible noodle shops. Your film is so full of *Alphaville, Blade Runner,* urban ennui. Is this your vision of the world? Dystopia?

WKW: No, but with *Chungking Express,* we had to do everything in two months' time. And we didn't have a script, because I had just finished *Ashes of Time,* which took two years to make. [*Ashes of Time*] was also my first time being a producer. And it was a costume film and involved a lot of actors and actresses. Everything was so expensive, and every decision you made, you had to be very careful because it cost a lot. From a director's point of view, I don't think [being the producer] was a good idea, because I had to think and think to make the decisions. The director needs to rely on his instinct, you know. The impulse. Then *Ashes of Time* was going to Venice that year, so we had a slot of two months' time without anything to do. So I said, "Why don't we make a film?" Like a student film, which is very simple, straightforward. With all of my crew. Like after taking a test, we would have a holiday. We spent two months making this film. And I had picked up some ideas when I was a scriptwriter, the Jacques Demy, the Cassavetes, things like that. So I just start shooting this film in chronological order. And I sat in the coffee shop writing during the day, and then shooting at night. We didn't have any permits, we didn't have any setups, we just went to places we already knew well. We worked like hell, like thieves, and it was fun. So the working style already dominated the look of the film. *Chungking Express* has "long legs," because we had to capture something outside as the actor and actress go in. Things like that. With *Fallen Angels,* the last scene, which is in the noodle shop, was shot on the first day. It was supposed to be the first day because at the time I wanted to tell the story backward. And so we went to that noodle shop—it is so small, the only way you can use it to shoot is with a wide-angle lens—but I felt that a wide-angle lens was quite ordinary. So I asked my cameraman, "Do we have an extra-wide-angle?" "Yes," he said. "We have a 6.8. But that will make your actress look terrible." I said, "Let's try it."

PB: Did you ask the actress first?

WKW: No. I didn't have to. And after that, after the first day, we saw that it was great. Because the perspective is totally different. It feels far away and yet so close. The people seem to be apart, but in fact they are very near. So actually it fits the content. Actually, we wanted to go even further, so we shot it in 1.66 ratio, in order to project it through an anamorphic lens, which is widescreen.

PB: To spread it out even more.

WKW: Yes, and I thought it looked good. And Hong Kong seemed to be ten times bigger. There was a lot of space, but I wasn't sure, and so I had it projected in a theater for myself, as a test. Every little move was so big on the screen that I realized it would be unbearable for the audience. So we just kept it the original way, which is the version you saw, projected in a normal way, not anamorphic. But we are trying to do it in a video version, where the image is smaller.

PB: There's also a lot of stuff you do with the optical printer as well. There's a sort of doubling of the image, where a head will appear and then a doubling of the head. I mean, the whole effect of this seems to be to get across that idea of disintegration. Is this your vision of things, of the future? Is this some kind of secret political reference to the handover of Hong Kong in 1997?

WKW: No. (Laughs.) I think it's all because of the moment. I want to capture the moment.

PB: Of these people's lives?

WKW: Some kind of moment.

PB: Or the moment of history? Do you mean this moment of history?

WKW: No no no.

PB: Just the event?

WKW: Yes, existence at that moment.

PB: Well, what knocked me out so much is that your camera moves around, and you have to pay attention every second, and then it will stop suddenly in a heartbreaking composition, when she has her head on his shoulder on the motorcycle, for example, at the very end. The way her head is very big in the foreground and all. I mean, those moments have a real power. But I was also wondering, is it fair to say that your films are ultimately about other films, rather than about real life?

WKW: They're about real life.

PB: Really?

WKW: Well, the formal elements are only the uniform, or the clothes, or the outfit. Like playing with other genres, it's like a game for us, just a joke. We are trying to do these kinds of things, yes, but for us it is only the starting point. What we are interested in, I think, is the people and Hong Kong. Before *Fallen Angels,* I always chose locations because they were appropriate, and that was it. But things change very fast in Hong Kong. The locations for my first two films have disappeared already. Even in *Chungking Express,* my fourth film, some locations have disappeared, changed into other things. Like the fast-food shop in *Fallen Angels,* the last one, when the boy meets the girl again—it was the main location for *Chungking Express*—it is totally different already. So in *Fallen Angels,* I was trying to include a location which I thought would disappear within a year or two, like the teahouse and restaurants where the killers went, and the place where he lives, things like that. The lifestyle of Hong Kong in certain periods, maybe the sixties or seventies or eighties . . . I'm trying to preserve it on film.

PB: It makes perfect sense, but I must say that when I saw the film, I did not think of something like neorealism. But I understand what you're saying, it's an attempt to document a certain reality.

WKW: I'm not a neorealist.

PB: No. But it's a curious form of documentation. In other words, what you're not interested in is a kind of surface realism, per se.

WKW: Right.

PB: It's more the spirit of the place, the feel of the place, the moment that you're talking about.

WKW: Because when we are taking about neorealism, we don't have killers usually.

PB: No, that's right, you have "the people."

WKW: Yes, they are a fiction, you know. They are just concepts. So we can't do that, we have to do it another way.

PB: Right, but you're obviously attracted by these killers too. I mean, they're sort of . . .

WKW: Well, one of the reasons is in Hong Kong, we always pre-sell to get our film financed, and for most Southeast Asian markets, they just want to have action. So they always ask, "Is it a cop story or a gangster story?" So you have to choose. One or the other.

PB: It's got to be one of them, though?

WKW: Yes. So with *Chungking Express,* I said, "It is a cop *and* a gangster story." We have gangsters, and we have cops. But it is not a gangster/cop story. It is just about their lives, and that's it.

PB: So it's first of all financial.

WKW: Yes.

PB: Second of all, it's like when Godard used to say he would pick the worst possible novel to adapt for films.

WKW: Yes, and then try to do something else.

PB: Yes, a genre novel, and then try to do other things involved with it. Well, I'm just finishing a book on Antonioni, and what I'm trying to talk about . . .

WKW: Antonioni's great. And I learned one thing from Antonioni, he told me, sometimes the main character is not the actors and actresses, it's the background. Like *Eclipse. Eclipse* is one of my favorite movies.

PB: I think it's his best.

WKW: The last ten minutes is great. And it influenced me a lot, that ten minutes.

PB: Ah, that's good to hear, because when I was watching your film, I was thinking of Antonioni, and I said that to somebody, and they said, "Antonioni? You must be crazy." But it's the formal, the idea that abstract lines, and forms, and shapes, and colors can give emotional meaning and expression as much as narrative lines, dialogue, characters. That's what I saw. Yeah the last, what is it, seventeen minutes or something?

WKW: Yeah. It's about the place, not about the people. It's about the activities. It's great, and it was a new angle to me at that time when I was a student.

PB: How would you compare yourself to MTV? I think the comparison is superficial, but I can see someone saying to you, "I see you've watched a lot of MTV, everything is very fast, there's a lot of loud music, and so on." What would be your response to that?

WKW: Well, there's a lot of music in my films, and my editing's fast. But that's it, and I don't think my films are really like MTV. My first film was made in 1988, and it had to be a gangster film, because it was my first film. The producer said, "Okay, it's safe for you to make a gangster film." But by that time, we already had more than two hundred gangster films, and they were at their peak. So I said to myself, "Okay, since MTV's so popular, I'll borrow the form of MTV to make a gangster film, and see what happens."

PB: But you've obviously gone way beyond that now, because I've never seen anything on MTV . . . Well there's a care, for one thing, it takes a lot of time to make those images that you do.

WKW: But what I was thinking of at the time was that because gangster films are so vague, everything seems fake. Everybody has already said the same thing, and I didn't think people would believe it anymore. So I was trying to do it with the form of MTV, which just made it more fake, you know. You don't have the feeling that I'm trying to tell you a really serious story.

PB: Right. So it gets so fake, so totally artificial that a core of truth kind of comes out after all. A core of reality.

WKW: Yes.

PB: That's great. What are you working on now that you've finished *Fallen Angels*? Or are you going to rest for a while?

WKW: I have to work again soon. I'm now producing my own film, and I'm making . . . I don't think it's a musical, but I think it is kind of a rock opera, in Beijing, with the same boys and the same girls as *Chungking Express*.

PB: One last thing. Are you pretty comfortable with the takeover by mainland China of Hong Kong in 1997? Are you planning to leave the country, since your wife is American, or are you okay with the takeover?

WKW: Well, the change is already there. But nobody knows what will happen, not even the Chinese government. Because I don't think there's a previous example of something like this. And because of the uncertainty, everything seems so interesting and exciting to me. So I want to stay, and I think because of the changes some interesting stories will happen, and interesting films will be made. Not in 1997, but I think two years or three years later.

PB: I wonder if China is going to be more changed by Hong Kong than Hong Kong by China.

WKW: No.

PB: Don't you think that Hong Kong will have an immense effect on China?

WKW: No.

PB: Too small?

WKW: Yeah. Because China is so big. It's like a drop of water going back to the sea. Have you seen the article by Fred Dannen in *The New Yorker?*

PB: Yes, I read it, and I was going to ask you about that.

WKW: Well, I don't like the story because it's too dramatic. I have to call him . . .

PB: All the stuff about gangsters completely running the Hong Kong film industry?

WKW: Yes. But the title is good. It's called "Hong Kong Babylon." And Hong Kong cinema is like a Babylon. In fact, after 1949, Hong Kong has [always] had a special [meaning] for the people in China, because it was more modern. A very modern place, all the things from the western world, and you can live freely. And the people in China have had a love/hate relationship with it. They are kind of jealous, and they admire the lifestyle, things like that. So the music from Hong Kong, the movies from Hong Kong, the TV drama from Hong Kong did very well in China and went to all the big cities. And the singers and actors made a lot of money selling their photos and things like that. But I think after 1997, this uniqueness will disappear. It will be just another city in China.

PB: But I also believe somehow that capitalism is such a powerful, insidious force, because . . . How much influence has Hong Kong cinema and Hong Kong culture had on mainland China for the last thirty years, as you said so yourself? Forty years? A lot of influence, no?

WKW: That's true. And not only mainland China. Even people in the Chinatowns, in Europe, in America, and the whole Southeast Asian market. There's a lot of Chinese. And they are all influenced by Hong Kong culture.

Interview with Wong Kar-wai
(Cannes Film Festival, 2001)

The following interview took place before a packed audience at the 2001 Cannes International Film Festival under the rubric "Leçon de cinéma." It appears here in its entirety for the first time. The interview was conducted in English and has been silently edited for consistency in grammar and usage. Questions from the audience were entertained near the end of the discussion and have been included here as well. Prior to the interview, a short film entitled *In the Mood for Love 2001* was shown. The subject matter of the short was largely the same as that found in *In the Mood for Love*, but it takes place in a present-day convenience store. (Permission to publish this interview, from Gilles Ciment, the authorities at the Cannes Film Festival, and Jet Tone Productions, Wong Kar-wai's production company, is gratefully acknowledged.)

GILLES CIMENT: So this was not a sequel, but I think perhaps you should explain where this short film comes from in the birth of *In the Mood for Love*.

WONG KAR-WAI: Well, actually, when we started the project I wanted to make a film about food, so I called the project *Three Stories about Food,* which is the regional title of *In the Mood for Love.* The idea was to have three stories which described the way food affects people. The story happened in Chinese communities and was about Chinese people. Since the 1970s, I think there have been two inventions which have changed Chinese and Asian life in general. One is the rice cooker; the second one is instant noodles. It used to be that women would have to spend lots of time at home cooking for their families. Without the rice cooker you have to spend hours in the kitchen. After we got rice cookers, the women had more time for themselves.

And then, as in *In the Mood for Love,* people used to go out for noodles. It was like a family outing, because they lived in a very small space. So they needed an excuse to go out at night to have a cup of noodles. Actually, it wasn't the noodles, but they wanted to get some air. After we got instant noodles, people didn't go out for noodles anymore. And so the last story is about fast-food shops. We can see that a lot of people now, especially the young people, don't care about cooking. They prefer to go out.

The three stories are from different periods in Hong Kong, and we can see that the roles of men and women have changed a lot because of the habit of eating. The project actually has three stories, and the short film we've just seen is supposed to be the last one. It's like a dessert. We shot this short film in the first two days when we started our production. So it took only two nights, then we finished it, and then we worked on the main course, which is *In the Mood for Love.* But somehow *In the Mood for Love* became longer and longer, it has noodles and it has a rice cooker in it, but it became a film in itself. Actually, when the [Cannes] festival told me that I had to give a lesson here, I didn't have any lessons. I don't have anything to teach people because I don't think I'm a good example. We made a lot of mistakes. So I want to share my experience with you, and I think it's better to show you the way we make films and the process we have to go through. So we showed the short film in the festival.

GC: So this reveals a way of shooting film. Starting with three stories, which is kind of a habit in your career, or two or three parts. So this is the first thing, that you start shooting without real scripts, and you are writing during the shooting.

WKW: First of all, normally we shoot without a script, or without a real script or [even] a fake script, but we have an idea. My way of working has always started with short stories, because today I think that to make a film for ninety minutes there must be a lot of substance in it. I always have short film ideas, I don't know why, and we start with two or three stories. Sometimes it has only one.

GC: Like *Chungking Express,* for example.

WKW: Right, exactly.

GC: And sometimes you just forget the second one.

WKW: I don't forget it. Somehow it just becomes another film, like the relationship between *Chungking Express* and *Fallen Angels. Chungking Express* at first had three stories in it, but we finished two, and it was already a feature film. So we skipped the third one, and at the end we made another film called *Fallen Angels,* which is the third story of the original *Chungking Express* idea.

GC: Speaking of transmission and learning/teaching, what is strange is that you first learned graphic arts, and then you started working as a scriptwriter. Now that you're a director, you don't write scripts at all. So what kind of way through is this?

WKW: Well, actually, there are a lot of mistakes in it. The reason I studied graphic design at Hong Kong Polytechnic was because I thought that to be a graphic student you didn't have to write, and you didn't have to do a lot of homework. I had a friend who was a graphics student, and I admired his way of learning because they just went out to take pictures. It seemed very easy. But obviously it's not, and I'm not good in graphics. I don't have the patience to draw. So I became a writer because television in those days in Hong Kong had a training course for writers and directors. So I was trained as a writer, and I wrote scripts, but I hated writing. So I tried to be a director, and I thought, "Well, someone will write the script for me," but it didn't happen. You have to write the script by yourself. Even though we are shooting without a script—actually, at the end of the day we have a script. But it's only when the film is finished, [then] the script actually is very detailed.

GC: What's the difference for you between writing scripts for another director and writing a story for yourself?

WKW: [When you're] a writer, you know that when you finish the script, the director will turn the paper into images. And so, as a writer, you want to make sure that the film looks more or less the same as you imagined when you were writing. So you try to restrict the director in certain ways. You have a lot of dialogue in it, and you try to make it as precise as possible. But writing a script and directing it are different things. When I began directing, I always imagined myself as a director like Hitchcock, who was very well prepared and knew everything about his films. Very technical. But after the first day I realized that was the wrong idea because I would never be Hitchcock, since I changed [things] all the time. And also because I was the writer, I knew how to change it on set. So finally I said, "Why bother?" And also, you can't write all your images on paper, and there are so many things—the sound, the music, the ambience, and also the actors—when you're writing all of these details in the script, the script has no tempo, it's not readable. It's very boring. So I just thought, it's not a good idea [to write out a complete script beforehand], and I just wrote down the scenes, some essential details, and the dialogue. I give the rhythm of the scenes to the actors and skip all these technical things.

GC: The scripts you used to write for others, were they as labyrinthine as your films? Were they linear scripts, or the kind of scripts you now write for yourself?

WKW: I was a writer for eight years, so I wrote a lot of scripts. There are comedies, horror films, kung fu/martial art films, action films, all kinds of films. And I had a very good experience working with a director called Patrick Tam. He actually is one of the most important directors in the Hong Kong New Wave. He taught me a lot of things about directing and how to turn words into images. I wrote a script with him called *Final Victory,* and this was the first time that I realized that even with the same script, the film could look very different with different directors.

GC: Your first film was quite simple, with a simple and straight script. After that you developed a new way of deconstructing. What happened in your mind to change your way of telling stories?

WKW: Well, my first film [*As Tears Go By*] was made in 1988, the golden time in Hong Kong cinema. In that year, there were a lot of new filmmakers becoming directors because we were producing three hundred films a year in Hong Kong. In those days, Hong Kong films were financed by pre-selling the film to the traditional market, that is,

the Asian market. The producer needed only a story, a genre, and the name of the cast. The idea I had for a film was a gangster film. So we started as a gangster film, but somehow in the process of making the film I thought, "Well, I want to change this, and I want to change that." But this was my first film, so it was very difficult to change it. For the second film [*Days of Being Wild*], I had more tricks I wanted to do, and I knew how to change my script.

GC: So without a real script, what takes the place of the script? Is it music? Is it the music which helps you to explain things?

WKW: No, I don't want to give the wrong idea. Actually, we have a script. But the script is not in written form. Before you start a film you should have an idea of what the story is about. I'm quite experienced as a writer, so I know how the story should go. It's in my mind, but it's not written down as scene one, scene two, scene three . . . If you don't have a clue about the story, it will be very risky to make a film because you will waste a lot of time and effort.

GC: So in practice, what is your collaboration with the cinematographer or actors on the set without a written script?

WKW: Well, first of all, I think we are very lucky. We have been working with mostly the same crew since my first film, so it is a team that has worked together for fifteen years. And most of the actors and actresses know each other very well, so normally before we start shooting, I tell them the story will be like this, and the characters will be like that. And then we create the situations. When I was a writer, Hong Kong films were made like this because we had to produce the films in a month. So mostly, we had a story and we started shooting. But because we had to shoot in certain locations, we had to structure the films in a certain way that we could tell them, "We have scene twenty-one, scene four, and scene seventy-six in this place." We had to write all the scenes in that location, so we divided everything by locations instead of the numbers. It became a habit for me to know how many locations there were in my films and how we structured stories according to these locations.

GC: Which would not be very easy if you change during the shooting.

WKW: So you have more scenes in it. Then you [sometimes] have to find one more location to find the missing link.

GC: Do you rehearse with your actors?

WKW: No.

GC: And how many [takes]?

WKW: Well, it depends. When we start shooting we have to find the rhythm, so it's very slow. Every day can have ten or twelve setups. But when everybody's going in the same direction, the shooting actually moves very fast.

GC: What's the role of the music in the process of shooting and editing?

WKW: To me, music creates the rhythms. So if I want to explain to [director of photography] Chris Doyle the rhythm of the film, then I would play the CDs, play the music instead of showing him the script, because he wouldn't read the script anyway. It's very effective in a way, and also it helps me because I think the rhythm of the film is very important. So you have to get the rhythm, and then everything comes out slowly after that.

GC: So you are writing during the shooting, and also you are editing during the shooting. You don't divide the work step by step.

WKW: I don't have any patience, so I want everything to be done at the same time. You can also understand immediately whether it's the right rhythm or not. So whenever we find the rhythm, and we're just shooting and waiting until the end of production, then we start editing.

GC: And eventually you also start another film.

WKW: Of course. Actually, I'm always thinking about making films, sometimes a real movie, or like a circus in the old times. So we work together with a team, and then we can keep shooting. I have always dreamed of making ten films in eighteen months. You know, traveling along. People ask, "Do you ever take a vacation?" Making a film for me, the actual process of production, is a vacation. I enjoy the process very much.

GC: So that's why the shooting lasts so long?

WKW: Yeah, sometimes it's because you just fall in love with the film. You don't want to let go. Like *In the Mood for Love,* we made it longer and longer. We [originally] wanted to make the film end in the 1970s. So we just kept running, and at the end of the day we knew it was too much because we couldn't afford it, and so we had to stop. That doesn't mean the stories stop in my mind, because that story can go on forever. In the future maybe we can make that happen.

GC: So twice you started a new film during the shooting of a film—*Chungking Express* during *Ashes of Time,* and your next film *2046* you started during the shooting of *In the Mood for Love.* How can you manage to combine two films at the same time?

WKW: The experiences were different. The case with *Chungking Express* and *Ashes of Time* [happened] because we spent like two years making *Ashes of Time.* We finally finished the shooting, and we had our postproduction and editing [done], and we knew the film was going to the Venice Film Festival six months later. And during that time I thought, well, we have nothing to do, and I want to make a film which is very fast. I wanted to refresh myself. Because I knew if I stopped at *Ashes of Time,* it would take me two years to make another film, because that experience was quite terrible. I wanted to make a very simple film, just like a student film, and so we made *Chungking Express* in a month.

In the case of *In the Mood for Love* and *2046,* we didn't expect the Asian financial crisis. So we had to stop the production of *In the Mood for Love* because our financiers in Asia had problems. So we had to find the finances from Europe, and then we [started making] the film again. But because we had [also] committed to making the film *2046,* at a certain point we had to work on both films at the same time. That experience was really terrible because it was like falling in love with two women at the same time.

GC: And one is jealous of the other?

WKW: No, because whenever you are shooting *In the Mood for Love,* you are thinking about *2046.* And there are some locations—at first we went to Bangkok for *2046,* but in the whole process of looking for locations we found all of these places which we thought would be good for *In the Mood for Love.* So at the end, we had to move the production to Bangkok. And when we were shooting *2046,* we were thinking about *In the Mood for Love.* So it's very messy.

GC: I think everybody remembers that last year you finished *In the Mood for Love* at the last minute and came with your print to Cannes.

WKW: Well actually, I have to explain to you [turns to the audience] . . . Gilles, actually, was working with us, and I still remember the day when we got to Cannes because we were the last film showing in the festival. We arrived the day before the last day. Our print was still in Paris, [where they were] doing the electronic press kit. So even I hadn't seen the finished film. It was a terrible experience, but very exciting. But I don't want to try that again. And this year, Gilles was working on another film, the Hou Hsiao-hsien film, and he had the same experience. I think you should tell the audience about your experience dealing with directors like this.

GC: It's your fault, because I think you spoke with Hou Hsiao-hsien, and you told him that that was possible with us.

WKW: Well I think for directors, you spend two years making a film, of course you want to make sure of everything. And so you will wait until the last minute to make sure that it is the best you can do.

AUDIENCE MEMBER: I've been told that you actually shot footage [of the missing spouses in *In the Mood for Love*], and for the voice of the husband you were using Roy Cheung.

WKW: Yes, right. And actually, in some of the scenes, the husband, even though we can't see him, is Tony Leung himself. And in some scenes it is Maggie Cheung playing the role of the wife. At first I wanted to have all four characters in the film played by Maggie and Tony, both the wife and Mrs. Chan, and the husband and Mr. Chow.

AUDIENCE MEMBER: You spoke earlier about your dislike of scripts, or rather your preference for spontaneity on the set, and how you're not a Hitchcock [kind of] filmmaker because you were constructing things as you went along. One of the things I like most about *In the Mood for Love* was the way you slowly reveal the characters and the world within which they live. Both the art direction and the script are constructed like a crossword puzzle in some ways. There's so much left to the imagination, and there's so much that we don't get to see. It seemed to me that that was incredibly meticulously planned. Was that spontaneous? And how did you go about constructing that in the narrative?

WKW: The thing is, even though I know I can't be Hitchcock, I wanted to make a film like Hitchcock. So *In the Mood for Love* to me is actually like a thriller, a story with a lot of suspense. So we always kept the spouses, the husband and wife, somewhere outside of the frame. We can't see them, but there's always a kind of clue. The two [central] characters in the film want to know why, and they want to find out the truth. So it is a very typical Hitchcock story structure.

I always have to look for some music before we start shooting a film [to serve as a reference point]. We build the whole rhythm of the film so Chris Doyle knows how to dance with the camera. Because otherwise he would just do it like *Chungking Express.* I told him that this film was not *Chungking Express,* you have to be very quiet. You have to be very stable. Chris Doyle is like a jazz musician. We don't discuss the light, we don't discuss the camera angles, because we have worked together for more than ten years, and we know each other very well. For him, he needs to know the rhythm and the color of the film. The color is not actually the color red or blue, it's his feelings toward the film. And normally our process of working together, Chris, William [Chang, production designer], and me, is not always that I create the ideas and they follow them. Sometimes I will tell the story to William. I said, "Okay, the story is about two married couples, they're living in Hong Kong, they're from a Chinese background." So he creates the space, and then we react to the space. The way William works, he creates all of the existing light sources of the films. So when Chris walks into the space, he knows how to play with the lights and place his cameras. It's a very organic process.

AUDIENCE MEMBER: Can you talk about your first American film, *The Follow* [a six-minute short in a series of ads, called *The Hire,* sponsored by BMW and available on the Internet], which I believe premieres this week with Mickey Rourke and Forrest Whitaker, and how it was to work in L.A. with an American crew?

WKW: Actually, it's very interesting, because at first I wanted to make the film because they told me there's a script already. There's a script, and you shouldn't change the script. And so I thought, well, that's good, I don't have to write the script. I looked at the script, and it was very simple, and it had a lot of room for me to work on it. So I agreed to do it, and it took me only eight days. And I said, well, that's fine, it's like a vacation to me. So I go there with William [Chang], and we start shooting. At first we thought we should work like Hollywood directors. This is your role, that's my role, and I just follow the script. But the script had some problems, and the locations had problems. So we began to change the script, and we began to change the locations. So at the end I said to William, hey, we are doing the same thing that we did in Hong Kong. Even though every day on the set there's like thirty trucks. I don't know why, because we were only shooting two people. But there are thirty trucks, it's like a whole army. The way people make films in Hollywood, they have their structures, and they have a reason for them. If you are going to make huge movies, like fifty-million-dollar-budget movies, you have to work like this. In Hollywood there's a lot of people working on one thing, and they don't want to interfere with others. In Hong Kong, one person works on a lot of things. This is the difference. But if you are going to make very big movies, huge productions, you need structures like this so you can work very smoothly. If we were to use Hong Kong structures to make films like this it would create a lot of confusion and would be very messy. But if you are going to make a very personal film, a small film, I think the Hong Kong structure is better.

AUDIENCE MEMBER: [Speaking of the music,] you must go to the composer first, if you have the music ready to feed into the space when the space is ready.

WKW: Yes. This time [2046] it's much easier, because we have to deal with Wagner. We don't have to deal with Brian Ferry.

AUDIENCE MEMBER: Can you say anything more about the film?

WKW: Well, we wanted to make it as an opera because in opera there's always the structure, a stage work, act one, act two. And the theme of opera, most of the time, is promise and betrayal. The idea of 2046 is about promises. We had the idea for the film in 1997, when Hong Kong was going back to China, and the Chinese government promised Hong Kong fifty years unchanged. I think it is a big promise, so we wanted to make a film about that, and we wanted to see if there's anything that would change [over the next fifty years].

GC: So is it three stories again?

WKW: Yes, we have three acts.

GC: How is it to be your own producer? It's comfortable, of course, but is it also a problem in the process of making a film?

WKW: I think producing a film is a full-time job. So I have three full-time jobs by myself—writer, director, and producer. So I'm too slow. I can't make a lot of films. Also, it gives me a lot of freedom and responsibility. My first two films, there were a lot of people saying, "Okay, you can make the films that you want, but you don't care about the producers." And I said I'm going to be a producer myself, and I want to make sure I can survive.

GC: This morning, we saw "The Lesson" by André Delvaux. He spoke a lot about music in films. He says that he works a lot with music, and you are working a lot with music. Tell us something about music and your films.

WKW: Well, cinema is a mixture of sounds and images. Music is part of the sounds. To me, music can be used to describe a certain time, a certain period. Sometimes it can create colors. So if you are going to make a film now, about the contemporary world, you can still use music from different eras to put a color on it. I'm not so crazy about using music in a very functional way that follows the image. You know, whenever you have something very sad you have sad music, or when you're very happy you have exciting music. I think the music and the image actually have a kind of chemistry. I'm very interested in exploring this.

GC: What do you think about film school?

WKW: Actually, I didn't go to film school. I think spending some time in film school is good. You can see a lot of films. You can make some friends there. But honestly, I think you can't learn how to make a film in school. You have to learn how to make a film in daily life.

GC: How did you learn to make films? What films did you see when you were young and where?

WKW: My experience comes from my background. I was born in Shanghai, and I came to Hong Kong when I was five. Like those characters in *In the Mood for Love,* we were Shanghainese, and we didn't speak the local language. My mother liked movies a lot, so we spent almost every day watching films, different kinds of films. In Hong Kong we could see Hollywood films, Mandarin productions, local productions, European films. So actually, I think my advice to film students is, if you have a chance, see as many films as you can, bad films and good films. Good films can teach you something, and bad films can teach you something too.

GC: And I think that's a good place to conclude this interview.

WKW: Thank you very much.

[Interviews transcribed by Matt Condon and edited by Peter Brunette.]

(Note: Different ways of using one's given English and Chinese names in Hong Kong, plus different transcription systems from Chinese, make compiling a filmography for a Chinese director an exercise in creativity and hope. Further complicating matters is the fact that sometimes the titles of Hong Kong films are given in Mandarin, sometimes in Cantonese. What follows is the result of collating several different sources; it undoubtedly contains a host of errors, as do most lists of credits, in English, for Chinese films.)

Long feng zhi duo xing (Intellectual Trio; 1984)
Hong Kong
Director: Guy Lai
Writer: Wong Kar-wai

Shen yong shuang xiang pau xu ji (Rosa; 1986)
Hong Kong
Director: Tung Cho "Joe" Cheung
Writers: Barry Wong, Wong Kar-wai

Zui hou yi zhan (The Final Test; 1987)
Hong Kong
Director: Kin Lo
Writer: Wong Kar-wai

Zui hou sheng li (Final Victory; 1987)
Hong Kong
Director: Patrick Tam
Writers: Patrick Tam, Wong Kar-wai, Tsang Yu

Meng gui cha guan (The Haunted Cop Shop of Horrors; 1987)
Hong Kong
Director: Jeffrey Lau
Writer: Wong Kar-wai

Jiang hu long hu men (Dragon and Tiger Fight/Flaming Brothers; 1987)
Hong Kong
Director: Tung Cho "Joe" Cheung
Writer: Wong Kar-wai

Mongkok Carmen (As Tears Go By; 1988)
Hong Kong
Director: Wong Kar-wai
Writer: Wong Kar-wai
Producers: Rover Tang, Alan Tang (executive producer)
Cinematographer: Wai Keung Lau
Editor: Pi Tak Cheong
Production Design: William Chang
Music: Ting Yat Chung, Teddy Robin Kwan
Cast: Andy Lau (Wah), Maggie Cheung (Ngor), Jacky Cheung (Fly), Kau
    Lam (Kung), Alex Man (Tony), Ronald Wong (Site)

Meng gui xue tang (The Haunted Cop Shop of Horrors II; 1988)
Hong Kong
Distributor: Threat Theatre (video)
Director: Jeffrey Lau
Writer: Wong Kar-wai
Cast: Jacky Cheung (Kam Mark-K), Ricky Hui (Man-Chill), Charlie Cho
    (Nearsighted Vampire), Sandy Lam (Miss Bad Luck), Mei-guan Lau (Miss
    Spiritual), Billy Lau (Lazy-Bone), Jeffrey Lau (Cop), James Yi Lui (Ro-
    meo), Barry Wong (Senior Inspector), Fung Woo (Superintendent), Wong
    Kar-wai (Wong), Meg Lam (Sgt. Ming), Lan Law (Woman at Police Sta-
    tion)

A Fei Zhengzuan (Days of Being Wild; 1991)
Hong Kong
Production Company: In-Gear Film
Distributors: Golden Network Limited, Rim (U.S.)
Director: Wong Kar-wai
Assistant Director: JoAnn Cabalda-Banaga
Writer: Wong Kar-wai
Producers: Alan Tang (executive producer), Joseph Chan (associate produc-
    er), Rover Tang (producer)
Cinematographer: Christopher Doyle
Editors: Kai Kit-wai, Patrick Tam
Production Design: William Chang
Makeup: Tsang Ming-fai, Lo Shiu-lin

Cast: Leslie Cheung (Yuddy), Maggie Cheung (Su Li-zhen), Andy Lau (Tide), Carina Lau (Leung Fung-ying), Rebecca Pan (Rebecca), Jacky Cheung (Zeb), Danilo Antunes (Rebecca's Lover), Tony Leung Chiu-wai (Smirk)

Gauyat sandiu haplui (Saviour of Souls/Terrible Angel; 1992)
Hong Kong
Production Company: Team Work Production House
Directors: David Lai, Corey Yuen
Writer: Wong Kar-wai
Cinematography: Peter Pau
Editors: Kit-wai Kai, Hung Poon
Music: Dak-hei Bauu
Cast: Andy Lau (Ching), Anita Mui (Yiu May-kwan), Aaron Kwok (Silver Fox), Kenny Bee (Siu Chuen), Gloria Yip (Wai Heung), Carina Lau (Pet Lady), Henry Fong (Fox's Master)

Sediu yinghung tsun tsi dung sing sai tsau (The Eagle Shooting Heroes; 1993)
Hong Kong
Production Company: Jet Tone
Director: Jeffrey Lau
Writer: Louis Cha (novel)
Producers: Wong Kar-wai (executive producer), Sung-lin Tsai (producer)
Cinematographer: Peter Pau
Music: James Wong
Action Coordinator: Sammo Hung Kam-bo
Cast: Leslie Cheung (Wang Yao-shih), Brigitte Lin (Third Princess), Maggie Cheung (Imperial Master), Tony Leung Chiu-wai (Ouyang Feng), Tony Leung Kar-fai (Tuan Wang-yeh), Jacky Cheung (Hung Chi), Carina Lau (Chou Po-tung), Joey Wong (Wang's Sweetheart), Veronica Yip (Ouyang Feng's Cousin), Kenny Bee (Wang Chung-yang, the Taoist)

Dongzie Xidu (Ashes of Time; 1994)
Hong Kong
Production Company: Scholar Productions
Distributors: HKFM (U.S.)
Director: Wong Kar-wai
Writers: Wong Kar-wai, Louis Cha (novel, *The Eagle Shooting Heroes*)
Producer: Sung-lin Tsai
Cinematographer: Christopher Doyle
Editors: Kit-wai Kai, Patrick Tam
Production Design: William Chang

Costume Design: William Chang

Music: Frankie Chan

Action Sequence Designer: Sammo Hung Kam-bo

Cast: Brigitte Lin (Murong Yin/Murong Yang), Leslie Cheung (Ouyang Feng), Maggie Cheung (The Woman), Tony Leung Chiu-wai (Blind Swordsman), Jacky Cheung (Hong Qi), Tony Leung Kar-fai (Huang Yao-shi), Li Bai (Hong Qi's Wife), Carina Lau (Peach Blossom), Charlie Young (Young Girl), Shun Lau (Leader of Ouyang's Opponents in Opening Battle)

Chong qing sen lin (Chungking Express; 1994)

Hong Kong

Production Company: Jet Tone

Distributors: Miramax Films (U.S.), Rolling Thunder (U.S.)

Director: Wong Kar-wai

Assistant Directors: Zeng Shaoting, Jiang Yuecheng

Writer: Wong Kar-wai

Producers: Pui-wah Chan (executive producer), Yi-kan Chan (producer)

Cinematographers: Christopher Doyle, Wai Keung Lau

Editors: William Chang, Kit-wai Kai, Chi-leung Kwong

Production Design: William Chang

Production Supervisor: Jacky Pang

Art Director: Qiu Weiming

Visual Effects: Chiang Xiaolong

Special Effects: Deng Weijue, Ding Yunda

Costume Design: William Chang

Makeup: Zhenglin Li (hair stylist), Yuhao Wu (hair stylist), Guan Lina (make-up artist)

Music: Frankie Chan, Roel A. García

Cast: Brigitte Lin (Woman in Blonde Wig), Tony Leung Chiu-wai (Cop 633), Faye Wong (Faye), Takeshi Kaneshiro (He Qiwu, Cop 223), Valerie Chow (Air Hostess), Chen Jinquan (Manager of the Midnight Express), Guan Lina (Richard), Huang Zhiming (Man), Liang Zhen (The Second May), Zuo Songshen (Man)

Duo luo tian shi (Fallen Angels; 1995)

Hong Kong

Production Companies: Chan Ye-cheng, Jet Tone

Distributors: Electric, Kino International (U.S.)

Director: Wong Kar-wai

Assistant Director: Johhny Kwong

Writer: Wong Kar-wai

Producers: Wong Kar-wai (executive producer), Jacky Pang Yee Wah (executive producer), Norman Law (associate producer), Jeffrey Lau (producer)

Cinematographer: Christopher Doyle
Editors: William Chang, Ming Lam Wong
Production Design: William Chang
Production Managers: Carly Wong Tung Fa (executive production manager), Agnes Leung (assistant production manager), Jacky Pang Yee Wah (production manager)
Costume Design: William Chang
Makeup: Wu Xuhao (hair stylist), Lee-na Kwan (makeup artist)
Music: Frankie Chan, Roel A. García, Shirley Kwan
Sound: Cameron Hamza (sound mixer), Raymond Mak (sound mixer), Leung Tai (sound recordist), Cheng Xiaolong (sound effects)
Stunt Coordinator: Kin-kwan Poon
Cast: Leon Lai (Wong Chi-ming/Assassin), Michelle Reis (Dispatcher), Takeshi Kaneshiro (He Qiwu), Charlie Young (Charlie/Cherry), Karen Mok (Blondie/Baby), Fai-hung Chan (The Man Forced to Eat Ice Cream), Chen Man Lei (He Qiwu's Brother), Toru Saito (Sato), To-hoi Kong (Ah-hoi), Lee-na Kwan (Woman Pressed to Buy Vegetables), Yuk-ho Wu (Man Forced to Have His Clothes Washed)

Cheun gwong tsa sit (Happy Together; 1997)
Hong Kong
Production Companies: Block 2 Pictures (Hong Kong), Jet Tone, Prénom H (Japan), Seowoo Film Company (Hong Kong)
Distributors: Golden Harvest (Hong Kong), Kino International (U.S.)
Director: Wong Kar-wai
Assistant Director: Johhny Kwong
Writer: Wong Kar-wai
Producers: Wong Kar-wai (executive producer), Ye-cheng Chan (producer)
Cinematographer: Christopher Doyle
Editors: William Chang, Ming Lam Wong
Production Design: William Chang
Special Effects: Tom Cundom
Music: Danny Chung
Sound: Chi-tat Leung, Du-che Tu
Choreographer: Juan Carlos Copes
Cast: Leslie Cheung (Ho Po-wing), Tony Leung Chiu-wai (Lai Yiu-fai), Chen Chang (Chang), Gregory Dayton (Lover)

Choh chin luen hau dik yi yan sai gaai (First Love: A Litter on the Breeze; 1997)
Hong Kong
Production Companies: Amuse, Block 2 Pictures (Hong Kong), Jet Tone
Director: Eric Kot

Writers: Ocean Chan, Nianchen Ye
Producer: Wong Kar-wai
Cinematographer: Christopher Doyle
Editor: Kei-hop Chan
Production Design: Nin-chung Man
Music: Carl Wong
Cast: Calvin Choi, Takeshi Kaneshiro, Vincent Kok, Eric Kot, Sai Lan, Wai-wai Lee, Maggie Leung, Karen Mok

Dut yeung nin wa (In the Mood for Love; 2000)
Hong Kong
Production Companies: Block 2 Pictures (Hong Kong), Jet Tone, Paradis Films (France)
Distributor: USA Films (U.S.), Criterion Film Corporation (U.S.)
Director: Wong Kar-wai
Writer: Wong Kar-wai
Producers: Ye-cheng Chan (executive producer), William Chang (associate producer), Jacky Pang Yee Wah (associate producer), Wong Kar-wai (producer)
Cinematographers: Christopher Doyle, Pin Bing Lee
Editor: William Chang
Production Design: William Chang
Costume Design: William Chang
Music: Michael Galasso, Shigeru Umebayashi
Cast: Maggie Cheung (Mrs. Chan, née Su Li-zhen), Tony Leung Chiu-wai (Chow Mo-wan), Ping Lam Siu (Ah Ping), Tung Cho "Joe" Cheung (Special Appearance), Rebecca Pan (Mrs. Suen), Lai Chen (Mr. Ho), Man-lei Chan (Kam-wah Koo), Roy Cheung (Mr. Chan), Chi-ang Chi (The Amah), Hsien Yu, Po-chun Chow, Paulyn Sun

In the Mood for Love 2001 (2001)
Hong Kong
Production Company: Jet Tone
Distributor: Block 2 Pictures
Director: Wong Kar-wai
Writer: Wong Kar-wai
Producers: Chan Ye-chang (executive producer), Jacky Pang Yee-wah (Producer)
Editor: William Chang Suk-ping
Production Designer: William Chang Suk-ping
Music: Shigeru Umebayashi
Sound Effects: Tu Duu-chih

The Hire: The Follow
USA
Production Companies: Anonymous Content, BMW Films
Director: Wong Kar-wai
Writer: Andrew Kevin Walker
Producers: David Fincher (Executive Producer), Aristides McGarry (producer), Robert van de Weteringe Buys (producer)
Cinematographer: Harris Savides
Production Coordinator: Pamela Louise Griner
Storyboard Artist: Christopher Glass
Visual Effects Producer: Carla Attanasio
Music: Joel Goodman, Jeff Rona
Sound: Claude Letessier (supervising sound editor), Michel Henein (sound editor)
Video Assist Operator: David Presley
Cast: Clive Owen (The Driver), Mickey Rourke (The Husband), Adrianna Lima (The Wife), Forest Whitaker

Tian xia wu shuang (Chinese Odyssey; 2002)
Hong Kong
Director: Jeffrey Lau
Producer: Wong Kar-wai
Production Design: Tony Au
Costume Design: William Chang
Music: Frankie Chan, Roel A. García
Action Choreographer: Kin-kwan Poon
Cast: Tony Leung Chiu-wai (Dragon), Faye Wong (Emperor's Sister), Vicki Zhao (Phoenix), Chen Chang (Emperor), Roy Cheung, Eric Kot, Jing Ning, Rebecca Pan

2046 (2004)
Hong Kong
Production Company: Block 2 Pictures, Paradis Films, Orly Films
Director: Wong Kar-wai
Writer: Wong Kar-wai
Cinematography: Christopher Doyle, Lai Yiu Fai, Kwan Pung Leung
Costume Design: William Chang Suk Ping
Editor: William Chang Suk Ping
Sound: Claude Letessier, Tu Duu Chih
Cast: Chang Chen, Maggie Cheung, Takuya Kimura, Carina Lau, Tony Leung Chiu-wai, Faye Wong, Zhang Ziyi, Gong Li

Abbas, Ackbar. "The Erotics of Disappointment." In *Wong Kar-Wai.* Ed. Jean-Marc Lalanne, David Martinez, Ackbar Abbas, and Jimmy Ngai. 39–81. Paris: Editions Dis Voir, 1997.

Arthur, Paul. "*In the Mood for Love.*" *Cineaste* 26.3 (2001): 40–41.

Berry, Chris, ed. *Perspectives on Chinese Cinema.* London: British Film Institute Publishing, 1991.

Bordwell, David. "The Art Cinema as a Mode of Film Practice." *Film Criticism* 4.1 (1979): 56–65.

———. *Planet Hong Kong: Popular Cinema and the Art of Entertainment.* Cambridge, Mass.: Harvard University Press, 2000.

Browne, Nick, Paul G. Pickowicz, Vivian Sobchak, and Esther Yau, eds. *New Chinese Cinemas: Forms, Identities, Politics.* New York: Cambridge University Press, 1994.

Brunette, Peter, and David Wills. *Screen/Play: Derrida and Film Theory.* Princeton, N.J.: Princeton University Press, 1989.

Camhi, Leslie. "Setting His Tale of Love Found in a City Long Lost." *New York Times,* January 28, 2001, Arts and Leisure, 11, 26.

Carbon, J. "Indompte." *Positif* 410 (April 1995): 36–38.

Chew, Eugene. "Wong Kar-Wai and the West." *Toto: Cinema Matters.* June 6, 2001. <http://www.cse.unsw.edu.au/~peteg/zine/toto/wkw.htm>.

Chow, Rey. "Nostalgia of the New Wave: Structure in Wong Kar-Wai's *Happy Together.*" In *Keyframes: Popular Cinema and Cultural Studies.* Ed. Matthew Tinkcom and Amy Villarejo. 228–41. New York: Routledge, 2001.

———. *Primitive Passions: Visuality, Sexuality, Ethnography, and Contemporary Chinese Cinema.* New York: Columbia University Press, 1995.

Ciment, Michel. "Entretien avec Wong Kar-wai." *Positif* 410 (April 1995): 39–45.

———. "Wong Kar-Wai and Chinese Film." *Positif* 477 (November 2000): 72.

Ciment, Michel, and H. Niogret. "Entretien avec Wong Kar-Wai." *Positif* 442 (December 1997): 8–14.

————. "Entretien avec Wong Kar-Wai." *Positif* 477 (November 2000): 76–80. (A shorter version of this interview, in the original English, can be found on the bonus disc of the *In the Mood for Love* DVD [Criterion Collection, 2001]).

Codelli, L. "*In the Mood for Love.*" *Positif* 473–74 (July/August 2000): 101–2.

Dannen, Fredric, and Barry Long. *Hong Kong Babylon: An Insider's Guide to the Hollywood of the East.* New York: Miramax Books, 1997.

Doyle, Chris. "To the End of the World." *Sight and Sound* 7.5 (May 1997): 14–17.

Feuer, Jane. "Genre Study and Television." In *Channels of Discourse, Reassembled.* Ed. Robert C. Allen. 138–60. Chapel Hill: University of North Carolina Press, 1992.

Fu, Poshek, and David Desser, eds. *The Cinema of Hong Kong: History, Arts, Identity.* New York: Cambridge University Press, 2000.

Gross, Larry. "Nonchalant Grace." *Sight and Sound* 6.9 (September 1996): 6–10.

Hampton, H. "Blur as Genre." *Artforum* 34.7 (March 1996): 90–93.

In the Mood for Love. Dir. Wong Kar-wai. 2–disc DVD. Criterion Collection, 2001.

————. Press kit. USA Films, 2000.

Kaufman, Anthony. "Interview: The 'Mood' of Wong Kar-Wai: The Asian Master Does It Again." *indieWIRE.com.* February 2, 2001. <http://www.indiewire.com/film/interviews/int_Wong_Kar-Wai_010202.html>.

Lalanne, Jean-Marc. "Deux fois deux." *Cahiers du cinema* 490 (April 1995): 40–41.

————. "Images from the Inside." In *Wong Kar-Wai.* Ed. Jean-Marc Lalanne, David Martinez, Ackbar Abbas, and Jimmy Ngai. 9–27. Paris: Editions Dis Voir, 1997.

Lu, Sheldon Hsiao-peng. "Filming Diaspora and Identity: Hong Kong and 1997." In *The Cinema of Hong Kong: History, Arts, Identity.* Ed. Poshek Fu and David Desser. 273–88. New York: Cambridge University Press, 2000.

————, ed. *Transnational Chinese Cinemas: Identity, Nationhood, Gender.* Honolulu: University of Hawaii Press, 1997.

Marchetti, Gina. "Buying American, Consuming Hong Kong: Cultural Commerce, Fantasies of Identity, and the Cinema." In *The Cinema of Hong Kong: History, Arts, Identity.* Ed. Poshek Fu and David Desser. 289–313. New York: Cambridge University Press, 2000.

Ngai, Jimmy. "A Dialogue with Wong Kar-Wai." In *Wong Kar-Wai.* Ed Jean-Marc Lalanne, David Martinez, Ackbar Abbas, and Jimmy Ngai. 83–117. Paris: Editions Dis Voir, 1997.

Niogret, Hubert. "*As Tears Go By.*" *Positif* 341–42 (July/August 1989): 80.

————. "Entretien avec Christopher Doyle: 'L'expression visuelle d'une expérience émotionelle.'" *Positif* 442 (December 1997): 15–19.

Rayns, Tony. *"Ah Fei Zhenjuang (Days of Being Wild)."* *Sight and Sound* 4.12 (December 1994): 41–42.

———. "Charisma Express." *Sight and Sound* 10.1 (January 2000): 34–36.

———. *"Fallen Angels/Duoluo Tianshi."* *Sight and Sound* 6.9 (September 1996): 42.

———. "In the Mood for Edinburgh (An Interview with Wong Kar-Wai)." *Sight and Sound* 10.8 (August 2000): 14–17.

———. "Poet of Time." *Sight and Sound* 5.9 (September 1995): 12–16.

Reynaud, Bérénice. "Entretien avec Wong Kar-Wai." *Cahiers du cinéma* 490 (April 1995): 37–39.

———. *"Happy Together* de Wong Kar-Wai." *Cahiers du cinéma* 513 (May 1997): 76.

Rouyer, Philippe. *"In the Mood for Love:* Le secret magnifique." *Positif* 477 (November 2000): 74–75.

Siegel, Marc. "The Intimate Spaces of Wong Kar-Wai." In *At Full Speed: Hong Kong Cinema in a Borderless World.* Ed. Esther C. M. Yau. 277–94. Minneapolis: University of Minnesota Press, 2001.

Stephens, Chuck. "Time Pieces: Wong Kar-Wai and the Persistence of Memory." *Film Comment* 32.1 (January/February 1996): 12–18.

Stokes, Lisa Odham, and Michael Hoover. *City on Fire: Hong Kong Cinema.* New York: Verso, 1999.

Teo, Stephen. *Hong Kong Cinema.* London: British Film Institute Publishing, 1997.

Tsui, Curtis K. "Subjective Culture and History: The Ethnographic Cinema of Wong Kar-Wai." *Asian Cinema* 7.2 (1995): 93–124.

2046. Press kit. Block 2 Pictures, 2004.

Ungerböck, Andreas. "Melancolische Helden." *EPD Film* (June 1998): 24–29.

Yau, Esther C. M., ed. *At Full Speed: Hong Kong Cinema in a Borderless World.* Minneapolis: University of Minnesota Press, 2001.

43, 96; loneliness and isolation theme in, 47, 67; love theme in, 14, 18–19, 40–42, 77–78, 89, 100, 105; memory theme in, 20, 40–41; music and sound in, 12, 26–27, 40, 52–54, 94–95, 128, 130–33; political implications in, 14–15, 22, 43–45, 51–52, 75–77, 103, 120, 132; rejection theme in, 41–42; repetition and doubling motif in, 23, 48–51; slow-motion and stretch-print-ing technique in, 12, 39, 52, 61, 81–82; time and the past in, 12, 19–22, 39–40, 53–56, 79–80, 90–92, 100–105; visual techniques in, 52–53, 78–81, 88, 106–7, 116–17; voice-over technique in, 12, 27, 67–68, 74, 79, 93

Woo, John, 4

Zhang, Ziyi, 104–5

Peter Brunette is Reynolds Professor of Film Studies at Wake Forest University. He is the author of books on Roberto Rossellini and Michelangelo Antonioni and coauthor (with David Wills) of *Screen/Play: Derrida and Film Theory*.

Books in the series Contemporary Film Directors

Edward Yang
  John Anderson

Wong Kar-wai
  Peter Brunette

Claire Denis
  Judith Mayne

Joel and Ethan Coen
  R. Barton Palmer

Nelson Pereira dos Santos
  Darlene J. Sadlier

Abbas Kiarostami
  Mehrnaz Saeed-Vafa and
  Jonathan Rosenbaum

The University of Illinois Press
is a founding member of the
Association of American University Presses.

Composed in 10/13 New Caledonia
with Helvetica Neue display
by Jim Proefrock
at the University of Illinois Press
Designed by Paula Newcomb
Manufactured by Thomson-Shore, Inc.

University of Illinois Press
1325 South Oak Street
Champaign, IL 61820-6903
www.press.uillinois.edu

S: Have dialogue spoken over
macro close detailed images
of surfaces!
- Disconnect the voice from
the speaker! Either in
whole film or in M's
subjective experience
= This supports theme of
bringing surfaces to the
fore, and letting surfaces
reflect psychological
states!